**Ben Stacy Jerrik (Ed.)**

**Rick Hayes-Roth**

AF307124

**Ben Stacy Jerrik (Ed.)**

# Rick Hayes-Roth

## Chief technology officer, Hewlett-Packard, Edward Feigenbaum

**Part Press**

# Contents

## Articles



## References

# Rick_Hayes-Roth

<table>
<tr><td colspan="2" align="center">Frederick Hayes-Roth</td></tr>
<tr><td colspan="2" align="center"></td></tr>
<tr><td>Residence</td><td>California</td></tr>
<tr><td>Citizenship</td><td>U.S.</td></tr>
<tr><td>Fields</td><td>Information sharing: architecture, ontologies, services, and trust; Valuable Information at the Right Time (VIRT) services; Model-based communication networks; Semantic web technologies</td></tr>
<tr><td>Institutions</td><td>Naval Postgraduate School, Singularity University, Stanford University, Carnegie-Mellon University, The University of Michigan, MIT</td></tr>
<tr><td>Alma mater</td><td>PhD - Univ. of Michigan, 1974<br>MS - Univ. of Michigan, 1972<br>BA - Harvard University, 1969</td></tr>
<tr><td>Doctoral advisor</td><td>John Holland and Walter Reitman</td></tr>
<tr><td>Known for</td><td>Co-inventor of the Hearsay-II speech understanding system and blackboard architecture; expert systems industrialization; VIRT (smart push); and the Maritime Information Exchange Model (MIEM)[1]</td></tr>
<tr><td>Notable awards</td><td>Fellow, American Association of Artificial Intelligence</td></tr>
</table>

**Frederick Hayes-Roth** (born 1947) is an American computer scientist and educator. His principal work focuses on how to use computing processes to winnow data down to only those information items that are valuable to the receiver, using technology to deliver those items, and in designing IT systems structured for this task.

## Career

He was the Chief Technology Officer for Software at Hewlett-Packard from 2000-2001. Before that (1981-2000) he was Chairman and Chief Executive of two Silicon Valley companies which he co-founded. One was Teknowledge Corporation, founded with Edward Feigenbaum.[2]

He was the program director for research in Information Processing at the Rand Corporation from 1976-81. That research program was prolific and influential, leading to numerous systems and research paradigms, including the Opportunistic Model of Planning (one of the 10 most cited papers in Cognitive Science), the rule-based system ROSIE [3], a number of heuristic expert systems, Distributed Fleet Control, and methods for non-monotonic reasoning and learning in knowledge networks.

Prior to that (1976), was one of the co-inventors of the first continuous speech understanding systems, Hearsay-II,[4] which became the "blackboard architecture." [5]

Hayes-Roth held faculty positions at MIT, Stanford, and Carnegie Mellon. In 2003 he became a professor in the Information Sciences Department at the United States Navy's Naval Postgraduate School (NPS) in Monterey,

California. At NPS he has taught hundreds of mid-career leaders in DOD through his "capstone course" on IT Strategy and Policy at NPS. The focus of that course has been on ways to radically improve the success of DOD IT system efforts.[6]

Hayes-Roth's contributions have helped establish several methods and technologies now widespread in business and government for exploiting machine intelligence. Rule-based systems and expert systems routinely solve important problems and help organizations achieve higher levels of performance. His work on "Valued Information at the Right Time" (VIRT)[7] argues that "smart push" can increase communication efficiency by as much as five orders of magnitude. VIRT is used by the US Department of Defense and IT organizations such as Oracle.

Hayes-Roth promoted the idea of developing semantic models for information sharing based on their usefulness in end-to-end transactions. This approach has been pioneered in collaborative business areas such as electronics RosettaNet and mortgage processing MISMO. In the defense and security area, he has formulated a concept of "Rich Semantic Track" that would provide a standard formalized model of mobile entities with intention. Such a model would enable agencies to share information about aircraft or surface ships, for example, as well as their crews. In 2008, this work culminated in the release by the US Navy of the *Maritime Information Exchange Model* (MIEM).[8] The MIEM provides a semantic model, embodied in an XML schema, for tracking people, cargo, vessels, and facilities, as well as relationships among them including threats, anomalies, and other events. This research was featured in the National Research Laboratory (NRL) 2009 review.[1]

Through an interagency agreement, the MIEM became the maritime domain model within the National Information Exchange Model (NIEM). The NIEM is an interagency program led by DHS that provides information models to support collaborative sharing across federal, state, and local agencies.

Hayes-Roth is the originator of numerous patents [9], including patents on secure information exchange, change detection in web pages, and asynchronous phone communication.

In 2011, Hayes-Roth co-founded Truth Seal Corporation, a non-profit, in a response to the glut of information that makes it difficult to judge the veracity of information.[10] Truth Seal promotes truthfulness in public communications so that the general public uses credible information for judgments, decisions and actions. Truth Seal's intent is that market incentives will increase the quantity of truthful information that all consumers and citizens need to process.[11]

Hayes-Roth has written more than 100 frequently-cited, published papers and authored or co-authored five other books, *Building Expert Systems*; *Pattern-Directed Inference System*; *Radical Simplicity: Transforming Computers into Me-Centric Appliances*; *Hyper-Beings: How Intelligent Organizations Attain Supremacy through Information Superiority*; and *Truthiness Fever: How Lies and Propaganda are Poisoning Us and a Ten-Step Program for Recovery*. He started a blog also known as Truthiness Fever.

He is a Fellow of the Association for the Advancement of Artificial Intelligence, which cited him as follows:

> For leadership in commercialization of expert system technology; for the co-development of Hearsay II and opportunistic-planning; and for the technical management of ROSIE, M.1, S.1, and ABE.[12]

Hayes-Roth is also a Senior Member of the IEEE and a member of the Association for Computing Machinery.

## Notes


[1]  C. Dwyer, R. Hayes-Roth, D. Reading, and G. Small (2009). "A Maritime Information Exchange Model (MIEM) for Sharing Actionable
     Intelligence" (http://www.nrl.navy.mil/content_images/2009_NRL_Review(revised).pdf). *Naval Research Laboratory Review*: 169–171.

[2]  During this time as the EVP and Chief Scientist, he co-created the commercial field of Expert Systems, and was elected as a Fellow of AAAI
     for that work. He was also a co-founder of AAAI. Alex Roland, Philip Shiman (2002). *Strategic computing: DARPA and the quest for
     machine intelligence, 1983-1993* (http://books.google.com/books?id=eD4taFgeTUYC&pg=PA199). MIT Press. pp. 199–208.
     ISBN 978-0-262-18226-3. .

[3]  http://www.rand.org/pubs/papers/P7220.html

[4]  Erman, L.D.; Hayes-Roth, F.; Lesser, V.R.; Reddy, D.R. The HEARSAY-II Speech Understanding System: Integrating Knowledge to
     Resolve Uncertainty. *Computing Surveys*, Vol: 12, Num: 2, pp. 213 - 253 (http://mas.cs.umass.edu/pub/paper_detail.php/229)

[5]  An empirical investigation of the underlying behavioral processes of trip chaining (http://www.uctc.net/papers/694.pdf)

[6]  IS4182 (http://www.nps.edu/Academics/GeneralCatalog/414.htm#o1642)

[7]  Collected papers on VIRT. (http://faculty.nps.edu/fahayesr/virt.html)

[8]  Collected papers on the Maritime Information Exchange Model (MIFM) (http://faculty.nps.edu/fahayesr/miem.html)

[9]  http://www.google.com/search?tbm=pts&tbo=1&hl=en&q=hayes-roth&btnG=Search+Patents#pq=hayes-roth+f.&hl=en&cp=15&
     gs_id=4p&xhr=t&q=%22F.+Hayes-Roth%22&qe=IkYuIEhheWVzLVJvdGgi&qesig=OlAhS_zDvb93g61Q9h08Lg&
     pkc=AFgZ2tmeCLsmzwvk8TldOQjRyS6fU1F7RsLsTCAO2DRIflG-jwUXCe9HdVLDQq_U7h60tmP0IvH6EWidmutvfC6UtItGRcI6xA&
     pf=p&sclient=psy-ab&tbo=1&tbm=pts&source=hp&pbx=1&oq=%22F.+Hayes-Roth%22&aq=f&aqi=&aql=&gs_sm=&gs_upl=&
     bav=on.2,or.r_gc.r_pw.,cf.osb&fp=8413d2d84a5437fe&biw=1235&bih=781

[10]  "About" (http://www.truthseal.com/about). *TruthSeal website*. . Retrieved October 30, 2011.

[11]  Ubiquity Magazine, Volume 2011, Issue July 2011 (http://ubiquity.acm.org/article.cfm?id=2002437)

[12]  AAAI Fellows (http://www.aaai.org/Awards/fellows-list.php)


## References


Hayes-Roth, F., C. Blais, et al. (2008). How to Implement National Information Sharing Strategy (http://c4i.gmu.
edu/events/reviews/2008/papers/25_Hayes-Roth.pdf). AFCEA-GMU C4I Center Symposium: Critical Issues in
C4I, George Mason University, Fairfax, VA, AFCEA.

Hayes-Roth, F. and C. Blais (2008). "*A Rich Semantic Model of Track as a Foundation for Sharing Beliefs
Regarding Dynamic Objects and Events.*" Intelligent Decision Technologies **2**(1): 53-72.

Hayes-Roth, F. (2006). Model-Based Communication Networks and VIRT: Orders of Magnitude Better for
Information Superiority (http://ieeexplore.ieee.org/stamp/stamp.jsp?arnumber=4086616&isnumber=4043248).
MILCOM 2006, Washington, DC, IEEE.

Infoglut (http://faculty.nps.edu/fahayesr/docs/p15-denning-1.pdf), an ACM article by Peter Denning on VIRT.
*Communications of the ACM*, Volume 49, Issue 7 (July 2006).

"Honesty Is the Best Policy," *Ubiquity Magazine*, a publication of the ACM, Volume 2011 Issue July, July 2011.
Part One (http://ubiquity.acm.org/article.cfm?id=2002437). Part Two (http://ubiquity.acm.org/article.
cfm?id=2002438). Interviews with Rick Hayes-Roth.


## External links


*   NPS Faculty webpage (http://faculty.nps.edu/fahayesr/index.html)
*   NPS vita (http://research.nps.navy.mil/cgi-bin/vita.cgi?p=display_vita&id=1066256428)
*   *Truthiness Fever* (http://truthinessfever.com) blog
*   *Hyper-beings* (http://hyper-beings.com)
*   *Radical Simplicity* (http://www.amazon.com/dp/0131002910)
*   *Building Expert Systems* (http://www.amazon.com/dp/0201106868)
*   *Pattern-Directed Inference Systems* (http://www.amazon.com/dp/0127375503)
*   Worldcat (http://worldcat.org/identities/lccn-n77-13407)

# Chief_technology_officer

A **chief technology officer** (or **chief technical officer**; **CTO**) is an executive-level position in a company or other entity whose occupant is focused on scientific and technological issues within an organization. The role became prominent with the ascent of the information technology (IT) industry, but has since become prevalent in technology-based industries of all types (e.g. biotechnology, energy, etc.). As a corporate officer position, the CTO typically reports directly to the chief executive officer (CEO) and is primarily concerned with long-term and "big picture" issues (while still having deep technical knowledge of the relevant field). Depending on company structure and hierarchy, there may also be positions such as director of R&D and vice president of engineering whom the CTO interacts with or oversees. The CTO also needs a working familiarity with regulatory (e.g. U.S. Food and Drug Administration, Environmental Protection Agency, Consumer Product Safety Commission, as applicable) and intellectual property (IP) issues (e.g. patents, trade secrets, license contracts), and an ability to interface with legal counsel to incorporate those considerations into strategic planning and inter-company negotiations.

## Contrast with chief information officer (CIO)

The focus of a CTO may be contrasted with that of a CIO. A CIO is likely to solve organizational problems through acquiring and adapting existing technologies (especially those of an IT nature), whereas a CTO principally oversees development of *new* technologies (of various types). Many large companies have both positions.

Another major distinction is between technologies that a firm seeks to actually develop to commercialize *itself* vs. technologies that *support* or enable a firm to carry out its ongoing operations. A CTO is focused on technology integral to products being sold to customers or clients, while a CIO is a more internally oriented position focused on technology needed for running the company (and in IT fields, for maintaining foundational software platforms for any new applications). Accordingly, a CTO is more likely to be integrally involved with formulating intellectual property (IP) strategies and exploiting proprietary technologies.

In an enterprise whose primary technology concerns are addressable by ready-made technologies (which, by definition, is not the case for any companies whose very purpose is to develop *new* technologies), a CIO might be the primary officer overseeing technology issues at the executive level. In an enterprise whose primary technology concerns do involve developing (or marketing) new technologies, a CTO is more likely to be the primary representative of these concerns at the executive level.

## Contrast with chief science officer (CSO)

In some organizations, the CTO may also hold the chief science officer (CSO) title. Alternatively, a company could have one or the other, or both occupied by separate people. Often, a CSO exists in heavily research-oriented companies, while a CTO exists in product-development-focused companies. The typical category of research and development that exists in many science and technology companies could be led by either post, depending on which area is the organization's primary focus.

A CSO almost always has a basic or pure science background and an advanced degree, whereas a CTO often has a background in engineering - and possibly business development.

## Genesis of the CTO

In many older industries (whose existence may predate IT automation) such as manufacturing, shipping or banking, an executive role of CIO would often arise out of the process of automating existing activities; in these cases, any CTO-like role would only emerge if and when efforts would be made to develop truly novel technologies (either for facilitating internal operations or for enhancing products/services being provided), perhaps through "intrapreneuring."

## CTO of the United States

In March of 2012, Todd Park took over the role of Chief Technology Officer, after Aneesh Chopra had stepped down.

Previously, U.S. President Barack Obama appointed Chopra the United States' first chief technology officer in April 2009.

## References

2

- John Brockman, (not dated), "Nathan Myhrvold: The Chef". (http://www.edge.org/digerati/myhrvold/myhrvold_p1.html)
- Mary K. Pratt, "Is the CTO an R&D boss, a senior technologist, an IT visionary or a business insider? It depends." (http://www.computerworld.com/action/article.do?command=viewArticleBasic&articleId=276429) Computerworld.com
- Tom Berray & Raj Sampath, (2002), "The Role of the CTO, four models for success" (http://www.brixtonspa.com/Career/The_Role_of_the_CTO_4Models.pdf)
- R D Smith, (2003), "The Chief Technology Officer: Strategic responsibilities and relationships" (http://www.modelbenders.com/papers/SmithR_CTOStrategy.pdf)
- John W. Medcof and Haniyeh Yousofpourfard, (2006), "The CTO and Organizational Power and Influence" (http://www.iamot.org/conference/index.php/ocs/10/paper/view/1363/611)

# Hewlett-Packard

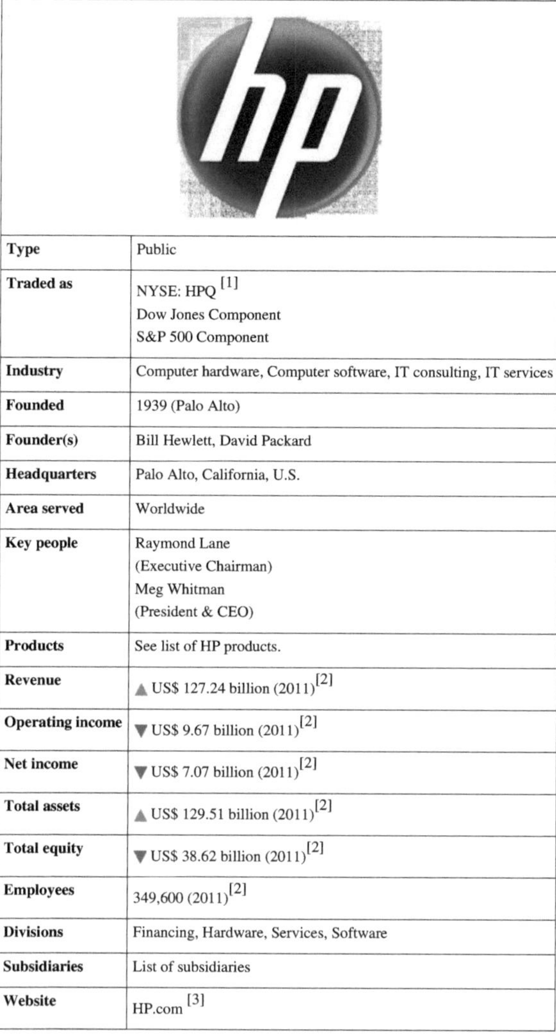

| Type | Public |
|---|---|
| Traded as | NYSE: HPQ [1]<br>Dow Jones Component<br>S&P 500 Component |
| Industry | Computer hardware, Computer software, IT consulting, IT services |
| Founded | 1939 (Palo Alto) |
| Founder(s) | Bill Hewlett, David Packard |
| Headquarters | Palo Alto, California, U.S. |
| Area served | Worldwide |
| Key people | Raymond Lane<br>(Executive Chairman)<br>Meg Whitman<br>(President & CEO) |
| Products | See list of HP products. |
| Revenue | ▲ US$ 127.24 billion (2011)[2] |
| Operating income | ▼ US$ 9.67 billion (2011)[2] |
| Net income | ▼ US$ 7.07 billion (2011)[2] |
| Total assets | ▲ US$ 129.51 billion (2011)[2] |
| Total equity | ▼ US$ 38.62 billion (2011)[2] |
| Employees | 349,600 (2011)[2] |
| Divisions | Financing, Hardware, Services, Software |
| Subsidiaries | List of subsidiaries |
| Website | HP.com [3] |

**Hewlett-Packard Company** (NYSE: HPQ [1]) or **HP** is an American multinational information technology corporation headquartered in Palo Alto, California, United States that provides products, technologies, software, solutions and services to consumers, small- and medium-sized businesses (SMBs) and large enterprises, including customers in the government, health and education sectors.

The company was founded in a one-car garage in Palo Alto by William (Bill) Redington Hewlett and Dave Packard. HP is the world's leading PC manufacturer. It specializes in developing and manufacturing computing, data storage, and networking hardware, designing software and delivering services. Major product lines include personal computing devices, enterprise, and industry standard servers, related storage devices, networking products, software and a diverse range of printers, and other imaging products. HP markets its products to households, small- to medium-sized businesses and enterprises directly as well as via online distribution, consumer-electronics and office-supply retailers, software partners and major technology vendors. HP also has strong services and consulting business around its products and partner products.

Major company events have included the spin-off of part of its business as Agilent Technologies in 1999, its merger with Compaq in 2002, and the acquisition of EDS in 2008, which led to combined revenues of $118.4 billion in 2008 and a Fortune 500 ranking of 9 in 2009.[4] In November 2009, HP announced the acquisition of 3Com,[5] with the deal closing on April 12, 2010.[6] On April 28, 2010, HP announced the buyout of Palm for $1.2 billion.[7] On September 2, 2010, HP won its bidding war for 3PAR with a $33 a share offer ($2.07 billion) which Dell declined to match.[8]

Hewlett-Packard is not affiliated with Packard Motor Car Corporation, founded by James Ward Packard and William Doud Packard, or with Packard Bell.

## History

Further information: List of Hewlett-Packard executive leadership

### Founding

Bill Hewlett and Dave Packard graduated with degrees in electrical engineering from Stanford University in 1935. The company originated in a garage in nearby Palo Alto during a fellowship they had with a past professor, Frederick Terman at Stanford during the Great Depression. Terman was considered a mentor to them in forming Hewlett-Packard.[9] In 1939, Packard and Hewlett established Hewlett-Packard (HP) in Packard's garage with an initial capital investment of US$538.[10] Hewlett and Packard tossed a coin to decide whether the company they founded would be called Hewlett-Packard or Packard-Hewlett[11] Packard won the coin toss but named their manufacturing enterprise the "Hewlett-Packard Company". HP incorporated on August 18, 1947, and went public on November 6, 1957.

Of the many projects they worked on, their very first financially successful product was a precision audio oscillator, the Model HP200A. Their innovation was the use of a small incandescent light bulb (known as a "pilot light") as a temperature dependent resistor in a critical portion of the circuit, the negative feedback loop which stabilized the amplitude of the output sinusoidal waveform. This allowed them to sell the Model 200A for $54.40 when competitors were selling less stable oscillators for over $200. The Model 200 series of generators continued until at least 1972 as the 200AB, still tube-based but improved in design through the years.

One of the company's earliest customers was Walt Disney Productions, which bought eight Model 200B oscillators (at $71.50 each) for use in certifying the Fantasound surround sound systems installed in theaters for the movie *Fantasia*.

## Early years

The company was originally rather unfocused, working on a wide range of electronic products for industry and even agriculture.

From the 1940s until well into the 1990s the company concentrated on making electronic test equipment: signal generators, voltmeters, oscilloscopes, frequency counters, thermometers, time standards, wave analyzers, and many other instruments. A distinguishing feature was pushing the limits of measurement range and accuracy; many HP instruments were more sensitive, accurate, and precise than other comparable equipment.

Following the pattern set by the company's first product, the 200A, test instruments were labelled with three to five digits followed by the letter "A". Improved versions went to suffixes "B" through "E". As the product range grew wider HP started using product designators starting with a letter for accessories, supplies, software, and components.

Original 1954
Hewlett-Packard
trademark

## The 1960s

HP is recognized as the symbolic founder of Silicon Valley, although it did not actively investigate semiconductor devices until a few years after the "Traitorous Eight" had abandoned William Shockley to create Fairchild Semiconductor in 1957. Hewlett-Packard's HP Associates division, established around 1960, developed semiconductor devices primarily for internal use. Instruments and calculators were some of the products using these devices.

HP partnered in the 1960s with Sony and the Yokogawa Electric companies in Japan to develop several high-quality products. The products were not a huge success, as there were high costs in building HP-looking products in Japan. HP and Yokogawa formed a joint venture (Yokogawa-Hewlett-Packard) in 1963 to market HP products in Japan.[12] HP bought Yokogawa Electric's share of Hewlett-Packard Japan in 1999.[13]

HP spun off a small company, Dynac, to specialize in digital equipment. The name was picked so that the HP logo "hp" could be turned upside down to be a reverse reflect image of the logo "dy" of the new company. Eventually Dynac changed to Dymec, then was folded back into HP in 1959.[14] HP experimented with using Digital Equipment Corporation minicomputers with its instruments, but after deciding that it would be easier to build another small design team than deal with DEC, HP entered the computer market in 1966 with the HP 2100 / HP 1000 series of minicomputers. These had a simple accumulator-based design, with registers arranged somewhat similarly to the Intel x86 architecture still used today. The series was produced for 20 years, in spite of several attempts to replace it, and was a forerunner of the HP 9800 and HP 250 series of desktop and business computers.

## The 1970s

The HP 3000 was an advanced stack-based design for a business computing server, later redesigned with RISC technology. The HP 2640 series of smart and intelligent terminals introduced forms-based interfaces to ASCII terminals, and also introduced screen labeled function keys, now commonly used on gas pumps and bank ATMs. The HP

Hewlett-Packard logo, mid-1970s

2640 series included one of the first bit mapped graphics displays that when combined with the HP 2100 21MX F-Series microcoded Scientific Instruction Set[15] enabled the first commercial WYSIWYG Presentation Program, BRUNO that later became the program HP-Draw on the HP 3000. Although scoffed at in the formative days of computing, HP would eventually surpass even IBM as the world's largest technology vendor, in terms of sales.[16]

"The new Hewlett-Packard 9100A personal computer is ready, willing, and able ... to relieve you of waiting to get on the big computer."

HP is identified by *Wired* magazine as the producer of the world's first marketed, mass-produced personal computer, the Hewlett-Packard 9100A, introduced in 1968.[17] HP called it a desktop calculator, because, as Bill Hewlett said, "If we had called it a computer, it would have been rejected by our customers' computer gurus because it didn't look like an IBM. We therefore decided to call it a calculator, and all such nonsense disappeared." An engineering triumph at the time, the logic circuit was produced without any integrated circuits; the assembly of the CPU having been entirely executed in discrete components. With CRT display, magnetic-card storage, and printer, the price was around $5000. The machine's keyboard was a cross between that of a scientific calculator and an adding machine. There was no alphabetic keyboard.

Steve Wozniak, co-founder of Apple, originally designed the Apple I computer while working at HP and offered it to them under their right of first refusal to his work, but they did not take it up as the company wanted to stay in scientific, business, and industrial markets.

The company earned global respect for a variety of products. They introduced the world's first *handheld scientific electronic calculator* in 1972 (the HP-35), the first *handheld programmable* in 1974 (the HP-65), the first *alphanumeric, programmable, expandable* in 1979 (the HP-41C), and the first symbolic and graphing calculator, the HP-28C. Like their scientific and business calculators, their oscilloscopes, logic analyzers, and other measurement instruments have a reputation for sturdiness and usability (the latter products are now part of spin-off Agilent's product line). The company's design philosophy in this period was summarized as "design for the guy at the next bench".

The 98x5 series of technical desktop computers started in 1975 with the 9815, and the cheaper 80 series, again of technical computers, started in 1979 with the 85.[18] These machines used a version of the BASIC programming language which was available immediately after they were switched on, and used a proprietary magnetic tape for storage. HP computers were similar in capabilities to the much later IBM Personal Computer, although the limitations of available technology forced prices to be high.

## The 1980s

In 1984, HP introduced both inkjet and laser printers for the desktop. Along with its scanner product line, these have later been developed into successful multifunction products, the most significant being single-unit printer/scanner/copier/fax machines. The print mechanisms in HP's tremendously popular LaserJet line of laser printers depend almost entirely on Canon's components (print engines), which in turn use technology developed by Xerox. HP develops the hardware, firmware, and software that convert data into dots for the mechanism to print. HP transitioned from the HP3000 to the HP9000 series minicomputers with attached storage such as the HP 7935 hard drive holding 404 MiB.

The garage in Palo Alto where Hewlett and Packard began their company

On March 3, 1986, HP registered the HP.com domain name, making it the ninth Internet .com domain ever to be registered.[19]

In 1987, the Palo Alto garage where Hewlett and Packard started their business was designated as a California State historical landmark.

## The 1990s

In the 1990s, HP expanded their computer product line, which initially had been targeted at university, research, and business users, to reach consumers.

HP also grew through acquisitions, buying Apollo Computer in 1989 and Convex Computer in 1995.

Later in the decade, HP opened hpshopping.com as an independent subsidiary to sell online, direct to consumers; in 2005, the store was renamed "HP Home & Home Office Store." [20]

Hewlett-Packard logo used until 2008

From 1995 to 1998, Hewlett-Packard were sponsors of the English football team Tottenham Hotspur.

In 1999, all of the businesses not related to computers, storage, and imaging were spun off from HP to form Agilent. Agilent's spin-off was the largest initial public offering in the history of Silicon Valley.[21] The spin-off created an $8 billion company with about 30,000 employees, manufacturing scientific instruments, semiconductors, optical networking devices, and electronic test equipment for telecom and wireless R&D and production.

In July 1999, HP appointed Carly Fiorina as CEO, the first female CEO of a company in the Dow Jones Industrial Average. Fiorina served as CEO during the technology industry downturn of the early 2000s. During her tenure, the market value of HP halved and the company incurred heavy job losses.[22] The HP Board of Directors asked Fiorina to step down in 2005, and she resigned on February 9, 2005.

## The 2000s

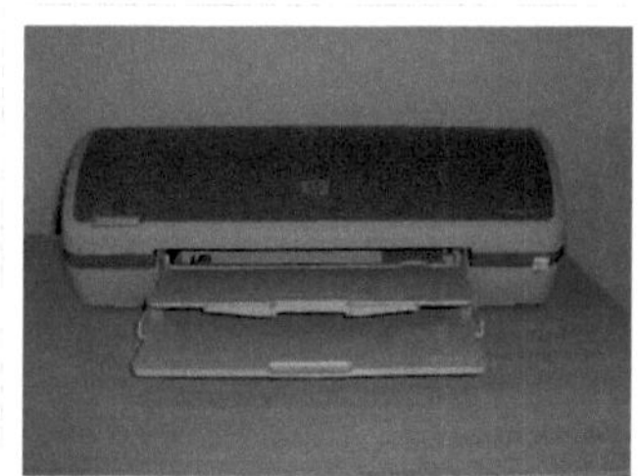
Hewlett-Packard Deskjet 3845 printer

The current two dimensional HP logo used on corporate documents, letterheads, etc.

On September 3, 2001, HP announced that an agreement had been reached with Compaq to merge the two companies.[23] In May, 2002, after passing a shareholder vote, HP officially merged with Compaq. Prior to this, plans had been in place to consolidate the companies' product teams and product lines.[24]

In 1998 Compaq had already taken over the Digital Equipment Corporation. That is why HP still offers support for PDP-11, VAX and AlphaServer.

The merger occurred after a proxy fight with Bill Hewlett's son Walter, who objected to the merger. Compaq itself had bought Tandem Computers in 1997 (which had been started by ex-HP employees), and Digital Equipment Corporation in 1998. Following this strategy, HP became a major player in desktops, laptops, and servers for many different markets. After the merger with Compaq, the new ticker symbol became "HPQ", a combination of the two previous symbols, "HWP" and "CPQ", to show the significance of the alliance and also key letters from the two companies **H**ewlett-**P**ackard and Compaq (the latter company being famous for its "Q" logo on all of its products.)

In the year 2004 HP released the DV 1000 Series, including the HP Pavilion dv 1658 and 1040 two years later in May 2006, HP began its campaign, *The Computer is Personal Again*. The campaign was designed to bring back the fact that the PC is a personal product. The campaign utilized viral marketing, sophisticated visuals, and its own web site (www.hp.com/personal). Some of the ads featured well-known personalities, including Pharrell, Petra Nemcova, Mark Burnett, Mark Cuban, Alicia Keys, Jay-Z, Gwen Stefani, and Shaun White.

On May 13, 2008, HP and Electronic Data Systems announced[25] that they had signed a definitive agreement under which HP would purchase EDS. On June 30, HP announced[26] that the waiting period under the Hart-Scott-Rodino Antitrust Improvements Act of 1976 had expired. "The transaction still requires EDS stockholder approval and regulatory clearance from the European Commission and other non-U.S. jurisdictions and is subject to the satisfaction or waiver of the other closing conditions specified in the merger agreement." The agreement was finalized on August 26, 2008, and it was publicly announced that EDS would be re-branded "EDS an HP company." As of September 23, 2009, EDS is known as HP Enterprise Services.

On November 11, 2009, 3Com and Hewlett-Packard announced that Hewlett-Packard would be acquiring 3Com for $2.7 billion in cash.[27] The acquisition is one of the biggest in size among a series of takeovers and acquisitions by technology giants to push their way to become one-stop shops. Since the beginning of the financial crisis in 2007, tech giants have constantly felt the pressure to expand beyond their current market niches. Dell purchased Perot Systems recently to invade into the technology consulting business area previously dominated by IBM. Hewlett-Packard's latest move marked its incursion into enterprise networking gear market dominated by Cisco.

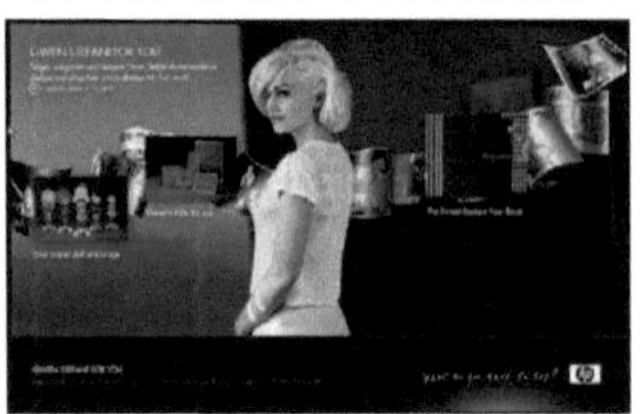

HP's recent campaign, *The Computer is Personal Again*, features several celebrity endorsements, including a TV commercial with Gwen Stefani.

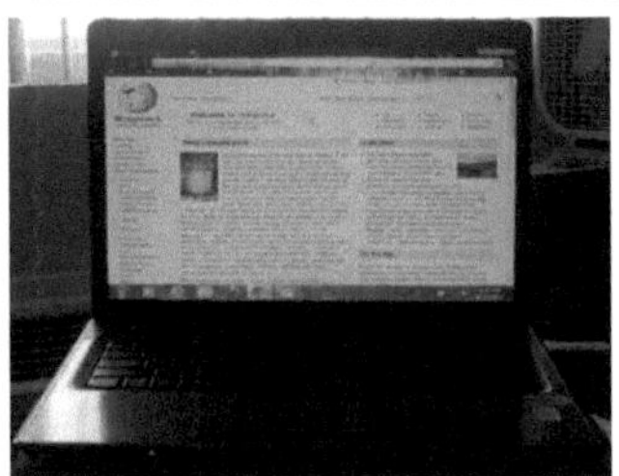

HP Presario F700 F767CL

## The 2010s

A Hewlett-Packard Mini 1000 netbook computer, a type of notebook computer

On April 28, 2010, Palm, Inc. and Hewlett-Packard announced that HP would be acquiring Palm for $1.2 billion in cash and debt,[28] In the months leading up to the buyout it was rumored that Palm was going to be purchased by either HTC, Dell, RIM or HP. The addition of Palm handsets to the HP product line provides some overlap with the current iPAQ mobile products but will significantly increase their mobile presence as those devices have not been selling well. The addition of Palm brings HP a library of valuable patents as well the mobile operating platform known as webOS. On July 1, 2010, the acquisition of Palm was final.[29] The purchase of Palm, Inc.'s webOS began a big gamble – to build HP's own ecosystem.[30] On July 1, 2011, HP launched its first tablet named HP TouchPad, bringing webOS to tablet devices. On September 2, 2010, HP won its bidding war for 3PAR with a $33 a share offer ($2.07 billion) which Dell declined to match. Following HP's acquisition of Palm, it would phase out the Compaq brand.

On August 6, 2010, CEO Mark Hurd resigned amid controversy and CFO Cathie Lesjak assumed the role of interim CEO. On September 30, 2010, Léo Apotheker was named as HP's new CEO and President.[31]

Apotheker's appointment sparked a strong reaction from Oracle chief executive Larry Ellison,[32] who complained that Apotheker had been in charge of SAP when one of its subsidiaries was systematically stealing software from Oracle. SAP accepted that its subsidiary, which has now closed, illegally accessed Oracle intellectual property.[33]

On August 18, 2011 HP announced that it would strategically exit the smartphone and tablet computer business, focusing on higher-margin "strategic priorities of cloud, solutions and software with an emphasis on enterprise, commercial and government markets"[34] They also contemplated spinning off their personal computer division into a separate company.[35] HP's consideration of a fundamental restructuring to quit the 'PC' business, while continuing to sell servers and other equipment to business customers, would have been similar to what IBM did in 2005.[36] However, after a brief review, HP decided their PC division was too integrated and critical to business operations, and the company reaffirmed their commitment to the Personal Systems Group.[37]

On September 22, 2011, Hewlett-Packard Co. named former eBay Inc. Chief Executive Meg Whitman its president and CEO, replacing Léo Apotheker, while Raymond Lane became executive chairman of the company.[38]

On March 21, 2012, HP said its printing and PC divisions would become one unit headed by Todd Bradley from the PC division. Printing chief Vyomesh Joshi is leaving the company.[39]

## Facilities

HP's global operations are directed from its headquarters in Palo Alto, California, USA. Its U.S. operations are directed from its facility in unincorporated Harris County, Texas, near Houston. Its Latin America offices in unincorporated Miami-Dade County, Florida, U.S., near Miami and in Medellín Colombia. Its Europe offices are in Meyrin, Switzerland, near Geneva. Its Asia-Pacific offices are in Singapore.[40] [41] [42] [43] [42] [44] [45] It also has large operations in Boise, Idaho, Roseville, California, Fort Collins, Colorado, San Diego, and Plano, Texas (the former headquarters of EDS, which HP acquired). In the UK, HP is based at a large site in Bracknell, Berkshire with offices in various UK locations, including a landmark office tower in London, 88 Wood Street. Its recent acquisition of 3Com will expand its employee base to Marlborough, Massachusetts.[46]

A sign marking the entrance to the HP corporate headquarters in Palo Alto, California

## Products and organizational structure

HP has successful lines of printers, scanners, digital cameras, calculators, PDAs, servers, workstation computers, and computers for home and small business use; many of the computers came from the 2002 merger with Compaq. HP today promotes itself as supplying not just hardware and software, but also a full range of services to design, implement, and support IT infrastructure.

HP's Imaging and Printing Group (IPG) is "the leading imaging and printing systems provider in the world for printer hardware, printing supplies and scanning devices, providing solutions across customer segments from individual consumers to small and medium businesses to large enterprises."[47] Products and technology associated with IPG include Inkjet and LaserJet printers, consumables and related products, Officejet all-in-one multifunction printer/scanner/faxes, Designjet and Scitex Large Format Printers, Indigo Digital Press, HP Web Jetadmin printer management software, HP Output Management suite of software, LightScribe optical recording technology, HP Photosmart digital cameras and photo printers, HP SPaM, and Snapfish by HP, a photo sharing and photo products service. On December 23, 2008, HP released iPrint Photo for iPhone a free downloadable software application that allows the printing of 4" x 6" photos.[48]

HP's Personal Systems Group (PSG) claims to be "one of the leading vendors of personal computers ("PCs") in the world based on unit volume shipped and annual revenue."[47] PSG includes business PCs and accessories, consumer

PCs and accessories, (e.g., HP Pavilion, Compaq Presario, VoodooPC), handheld computing (e.g., iPAQ Pocket PC), and digital "connected" entertainment (e.g., HP MediaSmart TVs, HP MediaSmart Servers, HP MediaVaults, DVD+RW drives). HP resold the Apple iPod until November 2005.[47]

HP Enterprise Business (EB) incorporates HP Technology Services, Enterprise Services (an amalgamation of the former EDS, and what was known as HP Services), HP Enterprise Security Services oversees professional services such as network security, information security and information assurance/ compliancy, HP Software Division, and Enterprise Servers, Storage and Networking Group (ESSN). The Enterprise Servers, Storage and Networking Group (ESSN) oversees "back end" products like storage and servers. HP's networking business unit ProCurve is responsible for the family of network switches, wireless access points, and routers.[49] They are currently a business unit of ESSN.

HP Software Division is the company's enterprise software unit. For years, HP has produced and marketed its brand of enterprise management software, HP OpenView. From September 2005 through 2010, HP purchased a total of 15 software companies between as part of a publicized, deliberate strategy to augment its software offerings for large business customers.[50] HP Software sells three categories of software: IT performance management, IT management software and information management software. HP Software also provides consulting, Software as a service, cloud computing solutions, education and support services.

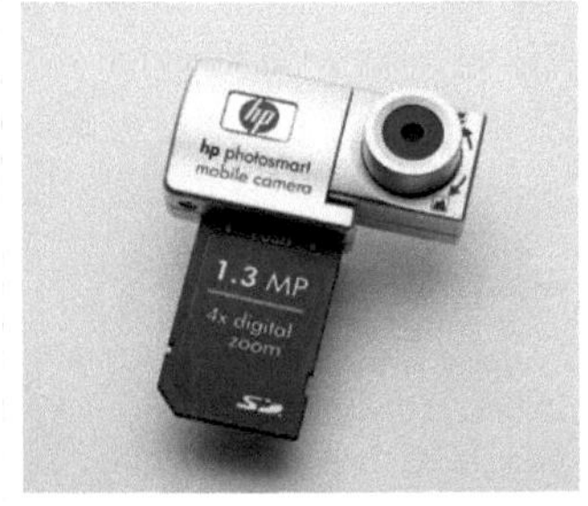

An HP camera with an SDIO interface, designed to be used in conjunction with a Pocket PC

HP's Office of Strategy and Technology[51] has four main functions: (1) steering the company's $3.6 billion research and development investment, (2) fostering the development of the company's global technical community, (3) leading the company's strategy and corporate development efforts,[52] and (4) performing worldwide corporate marketing activities. Under this office is *HP Labs*, the research arm of HP. Founded in 1966, HP Labs's function is to deliver new technologies and to create business opportunities that go beyond HP's current strategies. An example of recent HP Lab technology includes the Memory spot chip. *HP IdeaLab* further provides a web forum on early-state innovations to encourage open feedback from consumers and the development community.[53]

HP also offers managed services where they provide complete IT-support solutions for other companies and organisations. Some examples of these are: A large activity is HP offering "Professional Support" and desktop "Premier Support" for Microsoft in the EMEA marketplace. This is done from the Leixlip campus near Dublin, Sofia and Israel. Support is offered on the line of Microsoft operation systems, Exchange, Sharepoint and some office-applications.[54] But HP also offers outsourced services for companies like Bank of Ireland, some UK banks, the U.S. defense forces, etc.

## Corporate social responsibility

In July 2007, the company announced that it had met its target, set in 2004, to recycle one billion pounds of electronics, toner and ink cartridges.[55] It has set a new goal of recycling a further two billion pounds of hardware by the end of 2010. In 2006, the company recovered 187 million pounds of electronics, 73 percent more than its closest competitor.[56]

In 2008, HP released its supply chain emissions data — an industry first.[57]

In September 2009, *Newsweek* ranked HP No.1 on its 2009 Green Rankings of America's 500 largest corporations.[58] According to environmentalleader.com, "Hewlett-Packard earned its number one position due to its greenhouse gas (GHG) emission reduction programs, and was the first major IT company to report GHG emissions associated with its supply chain, according to the ranking. In addition, HP has made an effort to remove toxic substances from its products, though Greenpeace has targeted the company for not doing better."[59]

HP took the top spot on *Corporate Responsibility Magazine*'s 100 Best Corporate Citizens List for 2010.[60] The list is cited by *PR Week* as one of America's most important business rankings. HP beat out other Russell 1000 Index companies because of its leadership in seven categories including environment, climate changes and corporate philanthropy. In 2009, HP was ranked fifth.[61]

*Fortune* magazine named HP one of the World's Most Admired Companies in 2010, placing it No. 2 in the computer industry and No. 32 overall in its list of the top 50. This year in the computer industry HP was ranked No. 1 in social responsibility, long-term investment, global competitiveness, and use of corporate assets.[62]

In May 2011, HP released its latest Global Responsibility report covering accomplishments during 2010.[63] The report, the company's tenth, provides a comprehensive view of HP's global citizenship programs, performance, and goals and describes how HP uses its technology, influence, and expertise to make a positive impact on the world. The company's 2009 report won best corporate responsibility report of the year.[64] The 2009 reports claims HP decreased its total energy use by 9 percent compared with 2008. HP recovered a total of 118,000 tonnes of electronic products and supplies for recycling in 2009, including 61 million print cartridges.[65]

In an April 2010 *San Francisco Chronicle* article, HP was one of 12 companies commended for "designing products to be safe from the start, following the principles of green chemistry." The commendations came from Environment California, an environmental advocacy group, who praised select companies in the Golden State and the Bay Area for their efforts to keep our planet clean and green.[66]

In May 2010, HP was named one of the World's Most Ethical Companies by Ethisphere Institute. This is the second year in a row HP has made the list. Ethisphere reviewed, researched and analyzed thousands of nominations in more than 100 countries and 35 industries to create the 2010 list. HP was one of only 100 companies to earn the distinction of top winner and was the only computer hardware vendor to be recognized. Ethisphere honors firms that promote ethical business standards and practices by going beyond legal minimums, introducing innovative ideas that benefit the public.[67]

HP is listed in Greenpeace's Guide to Greener Electronics that ranks electronics manufacturers according to their policies on sustainability, energy and climate and green products. In November 2011, HP secured the 1st place (out of 15) in this ranking (climbing up 3 places) with an increased score of 5.9 (up from 5.5). It scored most points on the new Sustainable Operations criteria, having the best programme for measuring and reducing emissions of greenhouse gases from its suppliers and scoring maximum points for its thorough paper procurement policy.[68]

Moreover, HP does especially well for its disclosure of externally verified greenhouse gas emissions and its setting of targets for reducing them.[69] However, Greenpeace reports that HP risks a penalty point in future editions due to the fact that it is a member of trade associations that have commented against energy efficiency standards.[68]

HP has earned recognition of its work in the area of data privacy and security.[70] In 2010 the company ranked No. 4 in the Ponemon Institute's annual study of the most trusted companies for privacy.[71] Since 2006, HP has worked directly with the U.S. Congress, the Federal Trade Commission (FTC), and the Department of Commerce to establish a new strategy for federal legislation.[72] HP played a key role in work toward the December 2010 FTC report "Protecting Consumer Privacy in an Era of Rapid Change."[73]

After winning nine straight annual "Most Respected Company in China" awards from the Economic Observer and Peking University, HP China has added the "10 Year Contribution" award to its list of prestigious accolades. The award aims to identify companies doing business in China with outstanding and sustained performance in business operations, development and corporate social responsibility.[74]

## Brand

A Hewlett-Packard sponsored Porsche 997 GT3 Cup

The company sponsors the HP Pavilion at San Jose, home to the NHL's San Jose Sharks.

According to a Business Week Study, HP is currently the world's 11th most valuable brand.[75] Since its creation, the HP Logo has remained largely the same. Because of its extreme simplicity, the logo is recognized all over the world.

HP has many sponsorships. One well known sponsorship is of Walt Disney World's Epcot Park's Mission: SPACE.[76] From 1995 to 1999 they were the shirt sponsor of Premier League club Tottenham Hotspur F.C.. From 1997 to 1999 they were sponsors of Australian Football League club North Melbourne Football Club. They also sponsored the BMW Williams Formula 1 team until 2006 (a sponsorship formerly held by Compaq), and as of 2010 sponsor Renault F1. Hewlett-Packard also has the naming rights arrangement for the HP Pavilion at San Jose, home of the San Jose Sharks NHL hockey team.

After the acquisition of Compaq in 2002, HP has maintained the "Compaq Presario" brand on low-end home desktops and laptops, the "HP Compaq" brand on business desktops and laptops, and the "HP ProLiant" brand on Intel-architecture servers. (The "HP Pavilion" brand is used on home entertainment laptops and all home desktops.)[77]

HP uses DEC's "StorageWorks" brand on storage systems; Tandem's "NonStop" servers are now branded as "HP Integrity NonStop".[78]

## Legacy

Agilent Technologies, not HP, retains the direct product legacy of the original company founded in 1939. Agilent's current portfolio of electronic instruments are descended from HP's very earliest products. HP entered the computer business only after its instrumentation competencies were well-established. When Agilent was spun off, items in the Corporate Archives were split-up along product lines, with Agilent retaining almost all of the original HP archives — only where there was duplication of material, was HP given early Test and Measurement material. Both companies retained an original 200A Audio Oscillator.

## HP DISCOVER customer event

In 2011, HP Enterprise Business, along with participating independent user groups, combined its annual HP Software Universe, HP Technology Forum and HP Technology@Work into a single event, HP DISCOVER.[79] There are two HP Discover events annually, one for the Americas and one for Europe, Middle East and Africa (EMEA). HP DISCOVER 2011 Americas took place June 6–10, in Las Vegas at the Venetian/Palazzo.[80] The event offered nearly 1,000 sessions on application transformation, Converged Infrastructure, information optimization, mobile devices, webOS, global data centers, security, hybrid delivery and cloud computing.[81] Approximately 10,000 customers, partners and IT thought leaders attended HP Discover 2011 in Las Vegas and approximately 5,000 are expected to attend the EMEA event.[82] The Americas conference featured tracks designed for several industries including automotive and aerospace; communications, media & entertainment, energy, financial services, healthcare and life sciences, high tech and electronics, public sector, retail and consumer goods, and transportation and logistics. The nearly 1,000 sessions, hands-on labs and exhibits explored all areas of the HP Enterprise Business portfolio including servers, storage, networking, software and services.[83] In addition, the company provided sneak previews of its new tablet device, webOS TouchPad which will be available in July 1, 2011, starting at $500.[30] [84]

The HP DISCOVER 2011 event in EMEA is slated to take place in Vienna, Austria, at the Reed Exhibitions, Messe Wien Congress Center, on November 29 through December 1, 2011.[85]

# Controversies

## Spying Scandal

On September 5, 2006,David O'Neil and Shawn Cabalfin from *Newsweek* revealed that HP's general counsel, at the behest of chairwoman Patricia Dunn, contracted a team of independent security experts to investigate board members and several journalists in order to identify the source of an information leak.[86] In turn, those security experts recruited private investigators who used a spying technique known as pretexting.[87] The pretexting involved investigators impersonating HP board members and nine journalists (including reporters for CNET, the *New York Times* and the *Wall Street Journal*) in order to obtain their phone records. The information leaked related to HP's long-term strategy and was published as part of a CNET article[88] in January 2006. Most HP employees accused of criminal acts have since been acquitted.[89]

## Hardware

Hewlett-Packard has also been at the center of a fiasco in recent years. In November 2007, Hewlett-Packard released a BIOS update covering a wide range of laptops with the intent to speed up the computer fan as well as have it run constantly, whether the computer was on or off.[90] The reason was to prevent the overheating of defective NVIDIA graphics processing units (GPUs) that had been shipped to many of the original equipment manufacturers, including Hewlett-Packard, Dell, and Apple.[91] In July 2008, HP revealed an extension to the initial one-year warranty covering a few of the affected computers, but leaving many more without the protection, despite research showing that these computers were also affected.[92] Since this point, several websites have been documenting the issue, most notably www.hplies.com [93] and nvidiasettlement.com [94], a forum dedicated to what they refer to as Hewlett-Packard's "multi-million dollar cover up" of the issue. There have been several small-claims lawsuits filed in several states, as well as suits filed in other countries. Hewlett-Packard also faced a class-action lawsuit in 2009 over its i7 processor computers. The complainants stated that their systems locked up within 30 minutes of powering on, consistently. Even after being replaced with newer i7 systems, the lockups continued.[95]

### HP and Oracle lawsuit

On June 15, 2011, HP filed a lawsuit in California Superior Court in Santa Clara, claiming that Oracle had breached an agreement to support the Itanium microprocessor used in HP's high-end enterprise servers.[96] On June 15, 2011, HP sent a "formal legal demand" letter to Oracle in an attempt to force the world's No. 3 software maker to reverse its decision to discontinue software development on Intel Itanium microprocessor.[97]

## Notable people

- Michael Capellas (Compaq CEO/Chairman - HP President) [98]
- Rahul Sood (VoodooPC Founder) [99]
- Steve Jobs (Summer job) [100]
- Steve Wozniak (calculator designer) [101]

For *HP Chairmen and CEOs*.

## See also

- HP calculators
- HP Linux Imaging and Printing
- HP Software & Solutions
- HP User Group
- List of acquisitions by Hewlett-Packard
- List of computer system manufacturers
- List of Hewlett-Packard products

## References


[1] http://www.nyse.com/about/listed/quickquote.html?ticker=hpq

[2] "2010 Form 10-K, Hewlett-Packard Company" (http://www.sec.gov/Archives/edgar/data/47217/0001047469100104444/a2201180z10-k. htm). United States Securities and Exchange Commission. .

[3] http://www.hp.com/

[4] http://www.hp.com/hpinfo/newsroom/facts.html

[5] "San Jose Mercury News: "HP's acquisitions cement company's No. 1 status." Chris O'Brien. April 2010" (http://www.mercurynews.com/ opinion/ci_14893433?nclick_check=1). Mercurynews.com. . Retrieved 2011-11-30.

[6] "HP Completes Acquisition of 3Com Corporation, Accelerates Converged Infrastructure Strategy" (http://www.hp.com/hpinfo/newsroom/ press/2010/100412xa.html). Hewlett Packard. . Retrieved July 7, 2011.

[7] Vance, Ashlee; Wortham, Jenna (April 28, 2010). "H.P. to Pay $1.2 billion for Palm" (http://www.nytimes.com/2010/04/29/technology/ 29palm.html). *New York Times*. .

[8] "Dell gives up bidding war for 3Par Inc." (http://www2.journalnow.com/content/2010/sep/03/dell-gives-up-bidding-war-for-3par-inc/ business/). *Winston-Salem Journal*. Associated Press. September 3, 2010. . Retrieved September 3, 2010.

[9] Malone, Michael (2007). *Bill & Dave: How Hewlett and Packard Built the World's Greatest Company*. Portfolio Hardcover. pp. 39–41. ISBN 1-59184-152-6.

[10] "HP History: HP's Garage" (http://www.hp.com/hpinfo/abouthp/histnfacts/garage/). Hewlett Packard. December 6, 2005. . Retrieved July 7, 2011.

[11] "HP Company Information. HP Interactive Timeline" (http://www.hp.com/hpinfo/abouthp/histnfacts/timeline/). Hewlett Packard. . Retrieved July 7, 2011.

[12] "HP History : 1960s" (http://www.hp.com/hpinfo/abouthp/histnfacts/timeline/hist_60s.html). Hewlett Packard. March 17, 1961. . Retrieved July 7, 2011.

[13] Yokogawa Electric Corporation (July 7, 1999). "Yokogawa Electric Corporation and Hewlett-Packard Company Announce "Hewlett-Packard Japan to become Wholly Owned HP Subsidiary" HP and Yokogawa Sign Agreement" (http://www.yokogawa.com/pr/ Corporate/News/1999/pr-news-1999-03-en.htm). Yokogawa.com. . Retrieved July 7, 2011.

[14] "Dynac DY-2500 at HP Virtual Museum" (http://www.hp.com/hpinfo/abouthp/histnfacts/museum/earlyinstruments/0006/index. html). Hewlett Packard. . Retrieved July 7, 2011.

[15] "HP1000 F-Series" (http://www.hpmuseum.net/exhibit.php?hwdoc=110). HP Museum. . Retrieved July 7, 2011.

[16]  "Global 500 2009: Global 500 1-100 - FORTUNE on CNNMoney.com" (http://money.cnn.com/magazines/fortune/global500/2009/
       full_list/). CNN. July 20, 2009. . Retrieved May 9, 2010.

[17]  "Wired 8.12" (http://www.wired.com/wired/archive/8.12/mustread.html?pg=11). Wired.com. . Retrieved July 7, 2011.

[18]  "HP Computer Museum" (http://www.hpmuseum.net/exhibit.php?class=1&cat=9). HP Museum. . Retrieved May 9, 2010.

[19]  "Domain Timeline" (http://www.vb.com/domains-from-1986.htm). Vb.com. . Retrieved July 7, 2011.

[20]  http://www.shopping.hp.com/webapp/shopping/home.do

[21]  Arensman, Russ. "Unfinished business: managing one of the biggest spin-offs in corporate history would be a challenge even in the best of
       times. But what Agilent's Ned Barnholt got was the worst of times. (Cover Story)." Electronic Business 28.10 (Oct 2002): 36(6).

[22]  HP's share price moved from 45.36 to 20.14 during Fiorina's leadership, a performance of −56% (share price data from Bloomberg); the
       market as a whole, as measured by the benchmark Dow Jones U.S. Large Cap Technology Index (http://www.djindexes.com/mdsidx/
       index.cfm?event=showtotalMarketIndexData&perf=Historical Values), fell by 51% between July 19, 1999 and February 9, 2005.

[23]  "HP Press Release: Hewlett-Packard and Compaq Agree to Merge, Creating $87 billion Global Technology Leader" (http://www.hp.com/
       hpinfo/newsroom/press/2001/010904a.html). Hewlett Packard. . Retrieved May 9, 2010.

[24]  "HP Closes Compaq Merger" (http://www.hp.com/hpinfo/newsroom/press/2002/020503a.html) (Press release). Hewlett Packard. .
       Retrieved May 9, 2010.

[25]  "press release" (http://www.hp.com/hpinfo/newsroom/press/2008/080513a.html?jumpid=reg_R1002_USEN). Hewlett Packard. .
       Retrieved July 7, 2011.

[26]  "HP Announces Expiration of Waiting Period Under HSR Act" (http://www.hp.com/hpinfo/newsroom/press/2008/080630a.
       html?jumpid=reg_R1002_USEN) (Press release). Hewlett Packard. . Retrieved July 7, 2011.

[27]  "HP to Acquire 3Com for $2.7 billion" (http://www.hp.com/hpinfo/newsroom/press/2009/091111xa.html) (Press release). Hewlett
       Packard. . Retrieved May 9, 2010.

[28]  "HP to Acquire Palm for $1.2 billion" (http://www.hp.com/hpinfo/newsroom/press/2010/100428xa.html) (Press release). Hewlett
       Packard. . Retrieved May 9, 2010.

[29]  VentureBeat, Dean Takahashi. " HP Closes deal on $1.2B acquisition of Palm (http://mobile.venturebeat.com/2010/07/01/
       hp-closes-deal-on-1-2b-acquisition-of-palm/)." July 1, 2010.

[30]  Cliff Edwards and Aaron Ricadela, businessweek. " HP's Plan to Make TouchPad a Hit (http://www.businessweek.com/magazine/
       content/11_27/b4235040584134.htm)." Jun 23, 2011. Retrieved Jun 24, 2011.

[31]  "Léo Apotheker Named CEO and President of HP" (http://www.hp.com/hpinfo/newsroom/press/2010/100930c.html). Hewlett
       Packard. . Retrieved July 7, 2011.

[32]  "Larry Ellison outraged as HP hands top job to ex -SAP CEO" (http://www.computerworlduk.com/news/it-business/3242184/
       larry-ellison-outraged-as-hp-hands-top-job-to-ex--sap-ceo/). ComputerworldUK.com. . Retrieved July 7, 2011.

[33]  "SAP accepts some liability in Oracle lawsuit" (http://www.computerworlduk.com/news/applications/3234474/
       sap-accepts-some-liability-in-oracle-lawsuit/). ComputerworldUK.com. . Retrieved July 7, 2011.

[34]  "P Reports Third Quarter 2011 Results and Initiates Company Transformation" (http://h30261.www3.hp.com/phoenix.zhtml?c=71087&
       p=irol-newsArticle&ID=1598003&highlight=). HP.com. . Retrieved August 18, 2011.

[35]  Iwatani, Yukari (2011-08-19). "Pioneering Firm Bows to 'Post-PC World'" (http://online.wsj.com/article/
       SB10001424053111904070604576516770382416428.html?mod=mktw). Online.wsj.com. . Retrieved 2011-11-30.

[36]  "In nod to IBM, HP overhaul minimizes consumers" (http://finance.yahoo.com/news/In-nod-to-IBM-HP-overhaul-apf-707823588.
       html?x=0). August 18, 2011. .

[37]  "HP to Keep PC Division" (http://www.hp.com/hpinfo/newsroom/press/2011/111027xa.html). October 27, 2011. .

[38]  Agence France-Presse (September 22, 2011). "HP names Meg Whitman as CEO" (http://www.rawstory.com/rs/2011/09/22/
       hp-names-meg-whitman-as-ceo/). www.rawstory.com. . Retrieved September 24, 2011.

[39]  Brandon Bailey (March 22, 2012). "HP to combine PC, printing units" (http://www.newsobserver.com/2012/03/22/1949230/
       hp-to-combine-pc-printing-units.html). San Jose Mercury News. . Retrieved March 22, 2012.

[40]  "HP Online privacy statement" (http://welcome.hp.com/country/us/en/privacy.html#10). Welcome.hp.com. . Retrieved July 7, 2011.

[41]  "HP Office locations" (http://www.hp.com/country/us/en/contact/office_locs.html). Hewlett Packard. . Retrieved July 7, 2011.

[42]  http://welcome.hp.com/country/us/en/Worldwide_Dir5.pdf

[43]  " Plan de commune (http://www.meyrin.ch/jahia/webdav/site/meyrin/shared/documents/informations utiles/Plan Commune Meyrin.
       pdf)." Meyrin. Retrieved on September 29, 2009.

[44]  "HP Online privacy statement" (http://welcome.hp.com/country/us/en/privacy.html#10). Welcome.hp.com. . Retrieved May 9, 2010.

[45]  "HP Office locations" (http://www.hp.com/country/us/en/contact/office_locs.html). Hewlett Packard. . Retrieved May 9, 2010.

[46]  ""San Jose Mercury News: HP's acquisitions cement company's No. 1 status". Chris O'Brien. April 2010" (http://www.mercurynews.com/
       opinion/ci_14893433?nclick_check=1). Mercurynews.com. . Retrieved 2011-11-30.

[47]  http://www.shareholder.com/Common/Edgar/47217/1047469-05-28479/05-00.pdf

[48]  (http://www.hp.com/united-states/consumer/digital_photography/free/software/iprint-photo.html?jumpi=ex_r602_go/iprintphoto)

[49]  "HP ProCurve Networking – Network of Choice" (http://www.procurve.com). Procurve.com. . Retrieved July 7, 2011.

[50]  "HP Press release archives" (http://www.hp.com/hpinfo/newsroom/). Hewlett Packard. . Retrieved July 7, 2011.

[51]  "HP Executive Team Bios: Shane Robison" (http://www.hp.com/hpinfo/execteam/bios/robison.html). Hewlett Packard. . Retrieved
       July 7, 2011.

[52]  ProCurve Networking by HP – Features (http://www.hp.com/rnd/itmgrnews/hp_examines.htm)

[53]  "Title of backgrounder" (http://www.hp.com/hpinfo/newsroom/press_kits/2008/newhplabs/fs-newinitiatives.pdf) (PDF). . Retrieved July 7, 2011.

[54]  Wilcox, Joe (December 14, 2006). "HP-MS support deal" (http://www.microsoft-watch.com/content/business_applications/what_the_hpmicrosoft_deal_really_means.html). Microsoft-watch.com. . Retrieved July 7, 2011.

[55]  "HP Meets Billion Pound Recycling Goal Six Months Early, Sets Target for 2 billion Pounds by 2010" (http://www.mysolutioninfo.com/news-display.aspx?Code=1951&t=HP Meets Billion Pound Recycling Goal Six Months Early, Sets Target for 2 Billion Pounds by 2010). *My Solution Info*. . Retrieved July 16, 2007.

[56]  "Official HP Global Citizenship report 2009" (http://www.hp.com/hpinfo/globalcitizenship/pdf/fy09_brochure.pdf) (PDF). . Retrieved July 7, 2011.

[57]  "HP Steps Up IT Industry Transparency, Releases Supply Chain Emissions Data" (http://www.treehugger.com/files/2008/09/hp-steps-up-it-industry-with-carbon-emissions-report.php). . Retrieved October 21, 2009.

[58]  "Hewlett-Packard – Green Rating" (http://greenrankings.newsweek.com/companies/view/hewlett-packard). *Newsweek*. Newsweek, Inc.. . Retrieved September 22, 2009.

[59]  "HP, Dell, J&J, Intel and IBM Top Newsweek's Inaugural Green Rankings" (http://www.environmentalleader.com/2009/09/22/hp-dell-jj-intel-and-ibm-top-newsweeks-inaugural-green-rankings/). . Retrieved September 22, 2009.

[60]  "CR's 100 Best Corporate Citizens 2010" (http://www.thecro.com/files/CR100Best.pdf). theCRO.com. CRO Corp. Retrieved June 1, 2010.

[61]  Coster, Helen (March 3, 2010). "The 100 Best Corporate Citizens" (http://www.forbes.com/2010/03/02/100-corporate-citizens-leadership-citizenship-ranking.html). Forbes.com. Retrieved March 3, 2010.

[62]  "World's Most Admired Companies 2010: Hewlett-Packard snapshot" (http://money.cnn.com/magazines/fortune/mostadmired/2010/snapshots/206.html). FORTUNE on CNNMoney.com. March 22, 2010. Retrieved June 1, 2010.

[63]  "HP official corporate responsibility report 2010" (http://www.hp.com/hpinfo/globalcitizenship/). Hewlett Packard. . Retrieved July 7, 2011.

[64]  "Corporate Register News Release: "CR Reporting Awards Global Winners and Reporting Trends report released." March 24, 2011" (http://www.corporateregister.com/crra/help/CRRA11PressRelease.pdf) (PDF). . Retrieved July 7, 2011.

[65]  "HP Global Citizenship Report for 2009" (http://www.hp.com/hpinfo/globalcitizenship/pdf/fy09_brochure.pdf) (PDF). . Retrieved July 7, 2011.

[66]  Ross, Andrew S. (April 16, 2010). "State firms praised for purging toxic chemicals" (http://www.sfgate.com/cgi-bin/article.cgi?f=/c/a/2010/04/15/BUQP1CUR2T.DTL). San Francisco Chronicle.

[67]  "2010 World's Most Ethical Companies (http://ethisphere.com/wme2010/). Retrieved March 3, 2010.

[68]  "Guide to Greener Electronics" (http://www.greenpeace.org/international/en/campaigns/climate-change/cool-it/Guide-to-Greener-Electronics/). Greenpeace International. . Retrieved November 12, 2011.

[69]  "HP Global Citizenship: Product Manufacturing" (http://www.hp.com/hpinfo/globalcitizenship/09gcreport/enviro/energy/manufacturing.html). Hewlett-Packard. . Retrieved November 14, 2011.

[70]  Tsukayama, Hayley (March 15, 2011). ""Q&A with HP's Scott Taylor: Setting an industry privacy framework." Hayley Tsukayama. March 15, 2011" (http://www.washingtonpost.com/blogs/post-tech/post/qanda-with-hps-scott-taylor-setting-an-industry-privacy-framework/2011/03/14/AB33nrX_blog.html). *The Washington Post*. . Retrieved July 7, 2011.

[71]  "Ponemon News Release: "Ponemon Survey Names Twenty Most Trusted Companies for Privacy." Traverse City, Mich. February 26, 2010" (http://www.ponemon.org/news-2/26). Ponemon.org. . Retrieved July 7, 2011.

[72]  "FTC Second Roundtable Consumer Privacy. January 28, 2010" (http://www.safeinternet.org/events/ftc-second-roundtable-consumer-privacy). SafeInternet.org. . Retrieved July 7, 2011.

[73]  "U.S. Federal Trade Commission Staff Report:"Protecting Consumer Privacy in an Era of Rapid change." Dec. 2010." (http://www.ftc.gov/os/2010/12/101201privacyreport.pdf) (PDF). . Retrieved July 7, 2011.

[74]  "International Business Times: "2011 Most Respected Companies in China" Zoe Chan. April 23, 2011" (http://hken.ibtimes.com/articles/137375/20110423/award-ceremony-most-respected-companies-shenzhen.htm). Hken.ibtimes.com. April 23, 2011. . Retrieved July 7, 2011.

[75]  "100 Best Global Brands" (http://bwnt.businessweek.com/interactive_reports/best_global_brands_2009/index.asp). BusinessWeek.com. Retrieved June 1, 2010.

[76]  "Drawing in the audience" (http://www.hp.com/hpinfo/abouthp/sponsorships/ent.html). Hewlett Packard. . Retrieved April 23, 2011.

[77]  "HP United States – Computers, Laptops, Servers, Printers & more" (http://www.hp.com/). Hewlett Packard. . Retrieved July 7, 2011.

[78]  "Large Enterprise Business IT products, services, and solutions" (http://www.hp.com/country/us/en/solutions/leb.html). Hewlett Packard. . Retrieved July 7, 2011.

[79]  "HP Official Press Kit. June 6, 2011" (http://www.hp.com/hpinfo/newsroom/press_kits/2011/HPDiscover2011/index.html?mtxs=rss-corp-combined). Hewlett Packard. June 8, 2011. . Retrieved July 7, 2011.

[80]  Business Wire: "HP Unveils Premiere Client Event – HP Discover Americas, Nov. 16, 2010 (http://www.businesswire.com/news/home/20101116007511/en/HP-Unveils-Premiere-Client-Event—-HP)

[81]  "HP Unveils Premiere Client Event – HP Discover Americas; Attendee celebration concert to feature Paul McCartney" (http://www.hp.com/hpinfo/newsroom/press/2010/101116d.html?mtxs=rss-corp-combined) (Press release). Hewlett Packard. Nov. 16, 2010. . Retrieved July 7, 2011.

[82]  "Official HP Discover Event Web site" (https://h30406.www3.hp.com/campaigns/2010/events/discover/2011.php?jumpid=ex_r2548/
      us/jan15/ent/eb-ts/1-80GJ3/Discover_vanity). H30406.www3.hp.com. . Retrieved July 7, 2011.

[83]  HP Discover 2011 Las Vegas Session Catalog (https://h30496.www3.hp.com/scheduler/public.jsphttp://intranet.hp.com/tsg/ww3/
      HPDiscover/pages/home.aspx)

[84]  "Computing.co.uk. "HP Discover: Sneak look at HP's TouchPad." Dawinderpal Sahota. June 8, 2011" (http://www.computing.co.uk/ctg/
      news/2077192/hp-discover-sneak-look-hps-touchpad). Computing.co.uk. . Retrieved July 7, 2011.

[85]  "Taume.com: "HP Unveils Premier Client Event – HP DISCOVER EMEA." December 2, 2010" (http://news.taume.com/Technology/
      Industry/hp-unveils-premier-client-event-hp-discover-emea-18515). News.taume.com. December 2, 2010. . Retrieved July 7, 2011.

[86]  Suspicions and Spies in Silicon Valley | Newsweek Business|Newsweek.com (http://www.newsweek.com/id/45548/)

[87]  http://www.zdnet.com/news/faq-the-hp-pretexting-scandal/149452

[88]  Kawamoto, Dawn. "HP outlines long-term strategy |CNET News.com" (http://news.com.com/HP+outlines+long-term+strategy/
      2100-1014_3-6029519.html). News.com.com. . Retrieved July 7, 2011.

[89]  Katz, Leslie (March 31, 2007). "Calif. court drops charges against Dunn" (http://news.cnet.com/Calif.
      -court-drops-charges-against-Dunn/2100-1014_3-6167187.html). News.cnet.com. . Retrieved July 7, 2011.

[90]  "HP Limited Warranty Service Enhancement – HP Customer Care (United States – English)" (http://h10025.www1.hp.com/ewfrf/wc/
      document?lc=en&dlc=en&cc=us&docname=c01087277#c01087277_bios). H10025.www1.hp.com. . Retrieved May 9, 2010.

[91]  "All nvidia g84 and g86s are bad" (http://www.theinquirer.net/inquirer/news/1028703/nvidia-g84-g86-bad). The Inquirer. . Retrieved
      May 9, 2010.

[92]  {{cite web|url=http://h10025.www1.hp.com/ewfrf/wc/document?lc=en&dlc=en&cc=us&docname=c01300427 |title=HP Limited
      Warranty Service Enhancement (Product Numbers Included) – HP Customer Care (United States – English)
      |publisher=H10025.www1.hp.com |accessdate=May 9, 2010}}

[93]  http://www.hplies.com

[94]  http://www.nvidiasettlement.com/index.html

[95]  "Justia docket information *Kent v. Hewlett-Packard Company*" (http://dockets.justia.com/docket/california/candce/5:2009cv05341/
      221456/). Justia. . Retrieved October 28, 2010.

[96]  Jack Clark, ZDNet UK. " HP unleashes lawyers on Oracle over Itanium support (http://www.zdnet.co.uk/news/business-of-it/2011/06/
      16/hp-unleashes-lawyers-on-oracle-over-itanium-support-40093131/)." Jun 16, 2011. Retrieved Jun 17, 2011.

[97]  Poornima Gupta and Dan Levine, Reuters. " UPDATE 2-HP's latest lawsuit heightens rivalry with Oracle (http://www.reuters.com/
      article/2011/06/15/hp-oracle-lawsuit-idUSN1512123620110615)." Jun 15, 2011. Retrieved Jun 17, 2011.

[98]  "HP Press Release: Hewlett-Packard Announces Departure of Michael D. Capellas" (http://www.hp.com/hpinfo/newsroom/press/2002/
      021111b.html). Hp.com. . Retrieved 2011-11-30.

[99]  "HP Press Release: HP Completes VoodooPC Acquisition" (http://www.hp.com/hpinfo/newsroom/press/2006/061031b.
      html?jumpid=reg_r1002_usen). Hp.com. . Retrieved 2011-11-30.

[100]  "HP Retiree: Quotes and anecdotes About Bill Hewlett" (http://www.hp.com/retiree/history/founders/hewlett/quotes.html). Hp.com. .
       Retrieved 2011-11-30.

[101]  hpandwoz (2010-04-23). "Steve Wozniak Talks About HP" (http://www.youtube.com/watch?v=UMRmG72LBU8). YouTube. .
       Retrieved 2011-11-30.

## External links

- Official website (http://http://www.hp.com/)
- HP Printing and The Science Museum of Minnesota (http://h41186.www4.hp.com/country/us/en/lfs/)
- The Museum of HP Calculators (http://www.hpmuseum.org/)
- HP History Links (http://www.hpalumni.org/hp_history.htm)

Business data

- Hewlett-Packard Company (http://finance.google.com/finance?q=HPQ) at Google Finance
- Hewlett-Packard Company (http://finance.yahoo.com/q?s=HPQ) at Yahoo! Finance
- Hewlett-Packard Company (http://www.hoovers.com//--ID__10723--/free-co-factsheet.xhtml) at Hoover's
- Hewlett-Packard Company (http://www.reuters.com/finance/stocks/overview?symbol=HPQ) at Reuters
- Hewlett-Packard Company (http://google.brand.edgar-online.com/?sym=HPQ) SEC filings at EDGAR Online
- Hewlett-Packard Company (http://www.sec.gov/cgi-bin/browse-edgar?action=getcompany&CIK=47217)
  SEC filings at the Securities and Exchange Commission

# Edward_Feigenbaum

| Edward Albert Feigenbaum | |
|---|---|
| **Born** | January 20, 1936 |
| **Nationality** | American |
| **Fields** | Computer Science |
| **Institutions** | Stanford University |
| **Alma mater** | Carnegie Mellon University |
| **Doctoral advisor** | Herbert Simon |
| **Notable awards** | Turing Award |

**Edward Albert Feigenbaum** (born January 20, 1936; Weehawken, New Jersey) is a computer scientist working in the field of artificial intelligence. He is often called the "father of expert systems."

Feigenbaum completed his undergraduate degree (1956), and a Ph.D. (1960),[1] [2] at Carnegie Institute of Technology (now Carnegie Mellon University). In his Ph.D thesis, carried out under the supervision of Herbert Simon, he developed EPAM, one of the first computer models of how people learn.[3]

He received the ACM Turing Award, the most prestigious award in computer science, jointly with Raj Reddy in 1994 "For pioneering the design and construction of large scale artificial intelligence systems, demonstrating the practical importance and potential commercial impact of artificial intelligence technology". A former chief scientist of the Air Force, he received the U.S. Air Force Exceptional Civilian Service Award in 1997. In 1984 he was selected as one the initial fellows of the ACMI and in 2007 was inducted as a Fellow of the ACM. In 2011, Feigenbaum was inducted into IEEE Intelligent Systems' AI's Hall of Fame for the "significant contributions to the field of AI and intelligent systems".[4] [5]

He founded the Knowledge Systems Laboratory at Stanford University. He is currently a Professor Emeritus of Computer Science at Stanford University.

He was co-founder of several start-ups, such as IntelliCorp and Teknowledge. He was awarded the Fellow Award by the Computer History Museum in California in 2012.[6] [7]

## Articles by Edward Feigenbaum

- The Age of Intelligent Machines: Knowledge Processing--From File Servers to Knowledge Servers by Edward Feigenbaum [8]
- Feigenbaum, Edward A. (2003). "Some challenges and grand challenges for computational intelligence". *Journal of the ACM* **50** (1): 32–40. doi:10.1145/602382.602400.

## References


[1]  Edward Albert Feigenbaum (http://genealogy.math.ndsu.nodak.edu/id.php?id=61956) at the Mathematics Genealogy Project

[2]  "ProQuest Document ID 301899261" (http://ezproxy.lib.indiana.edu/login?url=http://search.proquest.com/docview/301899261?accountid=11620). *ProQuest Dissertations and Theses* (ProQuest). . Retrieved September 19, 2011

[3]  "Guide to the Edward A. Feigenbaum Papers" (http://cdn.calisphere.org/data/13030/hc/kt500039hc/files/kt500039hc.pdf). Stanford University. 2010. p. 2. . Retrieved September 12, 2011.

[4]  Error: Bad DOI specified!

[5]  "IEEE Computer Society Magazine Honors Artificial Intelligence Leaders" (http://www.digitaljournal.com/pr/399442). *DigitalJournal.com*. August 24, 2011. . Retrieved September 18, 2011. Press release source: *PRWeb* (Vocus).

[6]  Sweet, Carina (January 19, 2012). "The Computer History Museum Announces Its 2012 Fellow Award Honorees" (http://www.marketwatch.com/story/the-computer-history-museum-announces-its-2012-fellow-award-honorees-2012-01-19). *MarketWatch*. . Retrieved

January 30, 2012. "today announced its 2012 Fellow Award honorees: Edward A. Feigenbaum, pioneer of artificial intelligence and expert systems [...]"

[7] "Fellow Awards" (http://www.computerhistory.org/fellowawards/hall/bios/Edward,Feigenbaum/). Computer History Museum. . Retrieved January 30, 2012.

[8] http://www.kurzweilai.net/meme/frame.html?main=/articles/art0098.html

## External links

- Edward Albert Feigenbaum (http://genealogy.math.ndsu.nodak.edu/id.php?id=61956) at the Mathematics Genealogy Project
- Edward A. Feigenbaum (http://aigp.eecs.umich.edu/researcher/show/300) at the AI Genealogy Project (http://aigp.eecs.umich.edu/about).
- Edward Feigenbaum (http://ksl-web.stanford.edu/people/eaf/), Stanford Knowledge Systems, AI Laboratory
- Stanford Knowledge Systems, AI Laboratory (http://ksl.stanford.edu/)
- Oral history (http://purl.umn.edu/107283) interviews (http://purl.umn.edu/107282) with Edward Feigenbaum at Charles Babbage Institute, University of Minnesota, Minneapolis.

# RAND_Corporation

| | |
|---|---|
| **Founder(s)** | Henry H. "Hap" Arnold, Donald Wills Douglas, Sr. |
| **Type** | Global policy think tank |
| **Founded** | 1948 |
| **Location** | Santa Monica, California<br>Arlington, Virginia<br>Pittsburgh, Pennsylvania |
| **Origins** | United States Army Air Forces, Project RAND |
| **Key people** | Michael D. Rich |
| **Area served** | Predominantly United States of America |
| **Focus** | Policy Analysis |
| **Revenue** | $247.29 million (FY10)[1] |
| **Employees** | c. 1,700 |
| **Motto** | "To help improve policy and decisionmaking through research and analysis." |
| **Website** | www.rand.org [2] |

**RAND Corporation** (**R**esearch **AN**d **D**evelopment[3] ) is a nonprofit global policy think tank first formed to offer research and analysis to the United States armed forces by Douglas Aircraft Company. It is currently financed by the U.S. government and private endowment,[4] corporations[5] including the healthcare industry, universities[6] and private individuals.[7] The organization has long since expanded to working with other governments, private foundations, international organizations, and commercial organizations on a host of non-defence issues. RAND aims for interdisciplinary and quantitative problem solving via translating theoretical concepts from formal economics and the hard sciences into novel applications in other areas; that is, via applied science and operations research. Michael D. Rich is president and chief executive officer of the RAND Corporation.

RAND has approximately 1,700 employees and three principal North American locations: Santa Monica, California (headquarters); Arlington, Virginia; Pittsburgh, Pennsylvania. The RAND Gulf States Policy Institute[8] has offices in New Orleans, Louisiana, and Jackson, Mississippi. RAND Europe[9] is located in Cambridge, United Kingdom, and Brussels, Belgium. The RAND-Qatar Policy Institute[10] is in Doha, Qatar. RAND's newest offices are in Boston, Massachusetts, Abu Dhabi, The United Arab Emirates, and Mexico City, Mexico, a representative office.

RAND is also home to the Frederick S. Pardee RAND Graduate School, one of the original graduate programs in public policy and the first to offer a Ph.D. The program aims to have practical value in that students work alongside RAND analysts on real-world problems. The campus is at RAND's Santa Monica research facility. The Pardee RAND School is the world's largest Ph.D.-granting program in policy analysis.

RAND publishes *The RAND Journal of Economics*, a peer-reviewed journal of economics.

To date, 32 recipients of the Nobel Prize, primarily in the fields of economics and physics, have been involved or associated with RAND at some point in their career.[3] [11] [12]

## Project RAND

RAND was set up in 1946 by the United States Army Air Forces as **Project RAND**,[13] under contract to the Douglas Aircraft Company, and in May 1946 they released the *Preliminary Design of an Experimental World-Circling Spaceship*. In May 1948, Project RAND was separated from Douglas and became an independent non-profit organization. Initial capital for the split came from the Ford Foundation.

## History

Since the 1950s, the RAND has been instrumental in defining U.S. military strategy. Their most visible contribution is the doctrine of nuclear deterrence by Mutually Assured Destruction (MAD), developed under the guidance of then-Defense Secretary Robert McNamara and based upon their work with game theory.[14] Chief strategist Herman Kahn also posited the idea of a "winnable" nuclear exchange in his 1960 book *On Thermonuclear War*. This led to Kahn being one of the models for the titular character of the film *Dr. Strangelove*.[15] [16]

## Mission statement

RAND was incorporated as a non-profit organization to "further promote scientific, educational, and charitable purposes, all for the public welfare and security of the United States of America." Its self-declared mission is "to help improve policy and decision making through research and analysis", using its "core values of quality and objectivity."[3]

## Achievements and expertise

RAND Corporation, Pittsburgh, Pennsylvania

The achievements of RAND stem from its development of systems analysis. Important contributions are claimed in space systems and the United States' space program, in computing and in artificial intelligence. RAND researchers developed many of the principles that were used to build the Internet. RAND also contributed to the development and use of wargaming.

Current areas of expertise include: child policy, civil and criminal justice, education, health, international policy, labor markets, national security, infrastructure, energy, environment, corporate governance, economic development, intelligence policy, long-range planning, crisis management and disaster preparation, population and regional studies, science and technology, social welfare, terrorism, arts policy, and transportation.

RAND designed and conducted one of the largest and most important studies of health insurance between 1974 and 1982. The RAND Health Insurance Experiment, funded by the then-U.S. Department of Health, Education and Welfare, established an insurance corporation to compare demand for health services with their cost to the patient.

According to the 2005 annual report, "about one-half of RAND's research involves national security issues."

Many of the events in which RAND plays a part are based on assumptions which are hard to verify because of the lack of detail on RAND's highly classified work for defense and intelligence agencies.

The RAND Corporation posts all of its unclassified reports, in full, on its official website.

## Notable participants

- Stephen H Dole — Author of the pivotal book *Habitable Planets for Man*[18]
- Abram Shulsky — former Director of the Pentagon's Office of Special Plans[19]

## Criticism

In 1958, Democratic Senator Stuart Symington accused the RAND Corporation of defeatism for studying how the United States might strategically surrender to an enemy power. This led to the passage of a prohibition on the spending of tax dollars on the study of defeat or surrender of any kind. However, the senator had apparently misunderstood, as the report was a survey of past cases in which the U.S. had demanded unconditional surrender of *its* enemies, asking whether or not this had been a more favorable outcome to U.S. interests than an earlier, negotiated surrender would have been.[20]

John von Neumann, consultant to the RAND Corporation.[17]

## See also

- *A Million Random Digits with 100,000 Normal Deviates* (published by RAND)
- Pentagon Papers
- Lloyd Shapley
- Daniel Ellsberg
- Brookings Institution
- Council on Foreign Relations
- Hudson Institute
- Trilateral Commission
- Kepner-Tregoe
- Rational choice theory
- Amrom Harry Katz

## References

[1] *About the RAND Corporation — RAND at a Glance* (http://www.rand.org/about/glance.html), , retrieved 2009-02-09

[2] http://www.rand.org/

[3] The Rand Corporation. "History and Mission" (http://www.rand.org/about/history/). *RAND Corporation*. . Retrieved 2008-04-15.

[4] http://www.rand.org/about/glance.html RAND's private endowment

[5] http://www.rand.org/about/clients_grantors.html#industry Corporate contributors on RAND's website

[6] Major Clients and Grantors of RAND Research | RAND (http://www.rand.org/about/clients_grantors.html#colleges)

[7] http://www.rand.org/about/glance.html for RAND's individual contributions see Finance

[8] RAND Gulf States Policy Institute website (http://www.rand.org/rgspi/)

[9] RAND Europe website (http://www.rand.org/randeurope/)

[10] RAND-Qatar Policy Institute website (http://www.rand.org/qatar/)

[11] Brigette Sarabi, "Oregon: The Rand Report on Measure 11 is Finally Available" (http://www.safetyandjustice.org/info/or/story/631), *Partnership for Safety and Justice* (formerly *Western Prison Project*), January 1, 2005. Retrieved on April 15, 2008.

[12] Harvard University Institute of Politics. "Guide for Political Internships" (http://www.ksg.harvard.edu/iop/students_internships_db. php?action=id&id=551). Harvard University. . Retrieved 2008-04-18.

[13] RAND History and Mission (http://www.rand.org/about/history/). Accessed 13 April 2009.

[14] Twing, Steven W. (1998). *Myths, models & U.S. foreign policy* (http://books.google.co.uk/books?id=wS4A2jJph_cC&pg=PA163&dq). Lynne Rienner Publishers. ISBN 1555877664. .

[15] Hanks, Robert (19 December 2007). "The Week In Radio: The think tank for unthinkable thoughts" (http://www.independent.co.uk/
arts-entertainment/tv/reviews/the-week-in-radio-the-think-tank-for-unthinkable-thoughts-765975.html). *The Independent.* . Retrieved
2009-06-24.

[16] Kaplan, Fred (10 October 2004). "Truth Stranger Than 'Strangelove'" (http://www.nytimes.com/2004/10/10/movies/10kapl.
html?_r=1&pagewanted=1). *New York Times.* . Retrieved 2009-06-24.

[17] *Life Magazine*, 25th February 1957, *Passing of a Great Mind*, by Clay Bair JR. pages 89-104

[18] "Habitable Planets for man (6.4 MB PDF)" (http://rand.org/pubs/commercial_books/CB179-1/). RAND Corporation (free PDFs). .

[19] Seymour M. Hersh (12 May 2003). "Selective Intelligence — Donald Rumsfeld has his own special sources. Are they reliable?" (http://
www.newyorker.com/archive/2003/05/12/030512fa_fact). *The New Yorker.* .

[20] Poundstone, W. (1992). *Prisoner's Dilemma*. Doubleday.

# Further reading

## Books

- Alex Abella. *Soldiers of Reason: The RAND Corporation and the Rise of the American Empire* (2008, Houghton Mifflin Harcourt hardcover; ISBN 0-15101-081-1 / 2009, Mariner Books paperback reprint edition; ISBN 0-15603-344-5).

- S.M. Amadae. *Rationalizing Capitalist Democracy: The Cold War Origins of Rational Choice Liberalism* (2003, University Of Chicago Press paperback; ISBN 0-22601-654-4 / hardcover; ISBN 0-22601-653-6).

- Martin J. Collins. *Cold War Laboratory: RAND, the Air Force, and the American State, 1945-1950* (2002, Smithsonian Institution Scholarly Press hardcover, part of the Smithsonian History of Aviation and Spaceflight Series; ISBN 1-58834-086-4)

- Agatha C. Hughes and Thomas P. Hughes (editors). *Systems, Experts, and Computers: The Systems Approach in Management and Engineering, World War II and After* (2000, The MIT Press hardcover, part of the Dibner Institute Studies in the History of Science and Technology; ISBN 0-26208-285-3 / 2011, paperback reprint edition; ISBN 0-26251-604-7).

- Fred Kaplan. *The Wizards of Armageddon* (1983, Simon and Schuster hardcover, first printing; ISBN 0-67142-444-0 / 1991, Stanford University Press paperback, part of the Stanford Nuclear Age Series; ISBN 0-80471-884-9).

- Edward S. Quade and Wayne I. Boucher (editors), *Systems Analysis and Policy Planning: Applications in Defense* (1968, American Elsevier hardcover).

- Bruce L.R. Smith. *The RAND Corporation: Case Study of a Nonprofit Advisory Corporation* (1966, Harvard University Press / 1969; ISBN 0-67474-850-6).

- Mark Trachtenberg. *History and Strategy* (1991, Princeton University Press paperback; ISBN 0-69102-343-3 / hardcover; ISBN 0-69107-881-5).

## Articles

- Clifford, Peggy, ed. "RAND and The City: Part One" (http://www.smmirror.com/Volume1/issue19/
rand_and_the_city.html). *Santa Monica Mirror*, October 27, 1999 – November 2, 1999. Five-part series includes: 1 (http://www.smmirror.com/Volume1/issue19/rand_and_the_city.html); 2 (http://www.
smmirror.com/Volume1/issue20/rand_and_the_city.html); 3 (http://www.smmirror.com/volume1/issue21/
rand_and_the_city.html); 4 (http://www.smmirror.com/volume1/issue22/rand_and_the_city.html); & 5
(http://www.smmirror.com/Volume1/issue23/rand_and_the_city.html). Accessed 15 April 2008.

## External links

- Official website (http://www.rand.org)
- The Research and Development (RAND) Corporation (http://siarchives.si.edu/collections/siris_arc_217704) from the Smithsonian Institution Archives

# Blackboard_system

A **blackboard system** is an artificial intelligence application based on the blackboard architectural model, where a common knowledge base, the "blackboard", is iteratively updated by a diverse group of specialist knowledge sources, starting with a problem specification and ending with a solution. Each knowledge source updates the blackboard with a partial solution when its internal constraints match the blackboard state. In this way, the specialists work together to solve the problem. The blackboard model was originally designed as a way to handle complex, ill-defined problems, where the solution is the sum of its parts.

## Metaphor

The following scenario provides a simple metaphor that gives some insight into how a blackboard system works:

> A group of specialists are seated in a room with a large blackboard. They work as a team to brainstorm a solution to a problem, using the blackboard as the workplace for cooperatively developing the solution.
>
> The session begins when the problem specifications are written onto the blackboard. The specialists all watch the blackboard, looking for an opportunity to apply their expertise to the developing solution. When someone writes something on the blackboard that allows another specialist to apply their expertise, the second specialist records their contribution on the blackboard, hopefully enabling other specialists to then apply their expertise. This process of adding contributions to the blackboard continues until the problem has been solved.

## Components

A blackboard-system application consists of three major components

1. The software specialist modules, which are called knowledge sources (KSs). Like the human experts at a blackboard, each knowledge source provides specific expertise needed by the application.
2. The blackboard, a shared repository of problems, partial solutions, suggestions, and contributed information. The blackboard can be thought of as a dynamic "library" of contributions to the current problem that have been recently "published" by other knowledge sources.
3. The control shell, which controls the flow of problem-solving activity in the system. Just as the eager human specialists need a moderator to prevent them from trampling each other in a mad dash to grab the chalk, KSs need a mechanism to organize their use in the most effective and coherent fashion. In a blackboard system, this is provided by the control shell.

# Implementations

Famous examples of early academic blackboard systems are the Hearsay II speech recognition system and Douglas Hofstadter's Copycat and Numbo projects.

More recent examples include deployed real-world applications, such as the PLAN component of the Mission Control System for RADARSAT-1 [1], an Earth observation satellite developed by Canada to monitor environmental changes and Earth's natural resources.

GTXImage CAD software by GTX Corporation [2] was developed in the early 1990's using a set of rulebases and neural networks as specialists operating on a blackboard system.

Adobe Acrobat Capture (now discontinued) used a Blackboard system to decompose and recognize image pages to understand the objects, text, and fonts on the page. This function is currently built into the retail version of Adobe Acrobat as "OCR Text Recognition".

# See also

- Opportunistic reasoning
- Tuple spaces

# References

- Lee D. Erman, Frederick Hayes-Roth, Victor R. Lesser, and D. Raj Reddy, The Hearsay-II Speech-Understanding System: Integrating Knowledge to Resolve Uncertainty, Computing Surveys, 12(2):213-253, June 1980.
- Hayes-Roth, B. A blackboard architecture for control. Artificial Intelligence, 1985, 26, 251-321.
- Nii, H. P. Blackboard Systems. 1986.
- Iain Craig, Blackboard Systems. 1995.
- Daniel D. Corkill, Kevin Q. Gallagher, and Philip M. Johnson. Achieving flexibility, efficiency, and generality in blackboard architectures. In Proceedings of the National Conference on Artificial Intelligence, pages 18-23, Seattle, Washington, July 1987. Retrieve Article [3]
- Robert S. Engelmore and Anthony Morgan, editors. Blackboard Systems. Addison-Wesley, 1988.
- V. Jagannathan, Rajendra Dodhiawala, and Lawrence S. Baum, editors. Blackboard Architectures and Applications, Academic Press, 1989.
- Norman Carver. A Revisionist View of Blackboard Systems. In Proceedings of the 1997 Midwest Artificial Intelligence and Cognitive Science Society Conference, May 1997. Retrieve Article [4]
- Daniel D. Corkill. Blackboard Systems. AI Expert, 6(9):40-47, September, 1991. Retrieve Article [5]
- Daniel D. Corkill. Design Alternatives for Parallel and Distributed Blackboard Systems. In V. Jagannathan, Rajendra Dodhiawala, and Lawrence S. Baum, editors, *Blackboard Architectures and Applications*, pages 99–136, Academic Press, 1989. Retrieve Article [6]
- Daniel D. Corkill. Countdown to Success: Dynamic objects, GBB, and RADARSAT-1. Communications of the ACM, 40(5):48-58, May 1997. Retrieve Article [7]
- Daniel D. Corkill. Collaborating Software: Blackboard and Multi-Agent Systems & the Future. In Proceedings of the International Lisp Conference, New York, New York, October 2003. Retrieve Article [8]
- Daniel D. Corkill. GBBopen Tutorial. The GBBopen Project, March 2011. Retrieve PDF Article [9] Access on-line HTML hyperlink version [10]

## External links

- Open Blackboard System [11] An open source framework for developing blackboard systems.
- BBTech Corporation [12] A company that develops and maintains blackboard applications.
- GBBopen [13] An open source blackboard system framework.
- SQLBusRT [14] A blackboard implementation with temporal historical data added.
- Blackboard Event Processor [15] An open source blackboard implementation that runs on the JVM but supports plan scripting in JavaScript and JRuby.
- KOGMO-RTDB [16] A real-time open source blackboard for C/C++, used by some DARPA Urban Challenge autonomous vehicles.
- HarTech Technologies [17] A company that provides both Simulation and Command and Control solutions which are all based on a unique Blackboard architecture. The Blackboard development framework can be utilized to develop own costume applications.

## References

[1]  http://www.space.gc.ca/asc/eng/satellites/radarsat1/default.asp
[2]  http://www.gtx.com
[3]  http://dancorkill.home.comcast.net/pubs/aaai87.pdf
[4]  http://www.cs.siu.edu/~carver/ps-files/maics97.ps.gz
[5]  http://bbtech.com/papers/ai-expert.pdf
[6]  http://dancorkill.home.comcast.net/pubs/parallel-distributed-chapter.pdf
[7]  http://dancorkill.home.comcast.net/pubs/countdown.pdf
[8]  http://dancorkill.home.comcast.net/~dancorkill/pubs/ilc03.pdf
[9]  http://GBBopen.org/downloads/tutorial.pdf
[10]  http://GBBopen.org/hypertutorial/index.html
[11]  http://openbbs.sourceforge.net/
[12]  http://www.BBTech.com/
[13]  http://www.GBBopen.org/
[14]  http://sourceforge.net/projects/sqlbusrt/
[15]  http://code.google.com/p/blackboardeventprocessor/
[16]  http://www.kogmo-rtdb.de/
[17]  http://www.hartech.co.il/

# Naval_Postgraduate_School

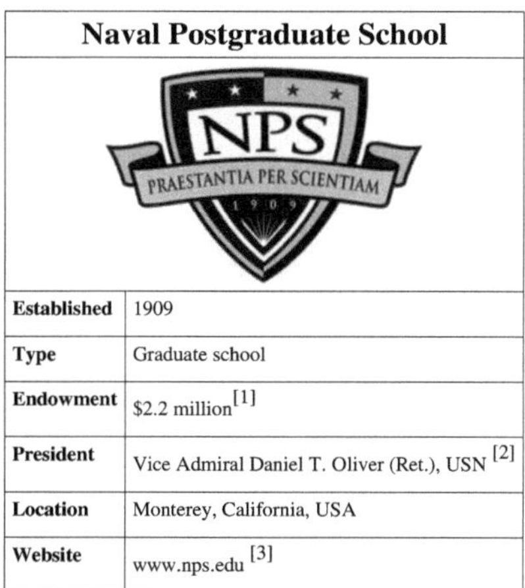

| Naval Postgraduate School | |
|---|---|
| **Established** | 1909 |
| **Type** | Graduate school |
| **Endowment** | $2.2 million[1] |
| **President** | Vice Admiral Daniel T. Oliver (Ret.), USN [2] |
| **Location** | Monterey, California, USA |
| **Website** | www.nps.edu [3] |

The **Naval Postgraduate School** (NPS) is an accredited research university operated by the United States Navy. Located in Monterey, California, it grants master's degrees, engineer's degrees and doctoral degrees. The school also offers research fellowship opportunities at the postdoctoral level through the National Research Council research associateship program.[4]

The NPS student population is mostly active-duty officers from all branches of the U.S. Military, although U.S. Government civilians and members of foreign militaries can also matriculate under a variety of programs. Most of the faculty are civilians.

The Air Force Institute of Technology (AFIT) serves a similar purpose. The United States Army does not have a similar institution, choosing instead to send its members to either NPS, AFIT or civilian institutions.

NPS and AFIT should not be confused with military Staff college or War College. The functions are significantly different. NPS and AFIT concentrate on topics traditionally associated with civilian graduate schools, focusing on their application to the military whereas Staff Colleges and War Colleges concentrate instead on staff functions, civil-military affairs, tactics and strategy.

Under a recent joint agreement between the Air Force and Navy, and codified by the 2005 Base Realignment and Closure Commission, AFIT and the Naval Postgraduate School have realigned their academic programs to reduce duplication, and both schools will be under the oversight of a common oversight panel. As an example of the consolidation, Navy officers are sent to learn aeronautical engineering at AFIT, while the Air Force officers learn meteorology at the Naval Postgraduate School.

Prior to being purchased by the U.S. Government, the school's campus was operated as the Del Monte Hotel. Some NPS buildings and the cactus garden date from that time.

# Academic structure

NPS offers graduate programs through four graduate schools and 12 departments. The different schools and departments each offer various PhD and M.S. level degrees:

- **Graduate School of Business & Public Policy** Web page [5], includes the following departments:

1. Acquisition Management
2. Enterprise Management
3. Financial Management
4. Management
5. Manpower and Economics
6. Operations and Logistics Management

- **Graduate School of Engineering & Applied Sciences** Web page [6], includes the following departments:

1. Applied Mathematics Department Web page [7]
2. Electrical and Computer Engineering Department Web Page [8]
3. Mechanical and Astronautical Engineering Department Web page [9]
4. Meteorology Department Web page [10]
5. Oceanography Department Web page [11]
6. Physics Department Web page [12]
7. Systems Engineering Department Web page [13]
8. Space Systems Academic Group Web page [14]
9. Navigation Systems Engineering Institute Web page [15]
10. Under Sea Warfare Systems Academic Committee Web page [16]
11. Remote Sensing Center Web page [17]
12. Spacecraft Robotics Laboratory Web page [18]

- **Graduate School of Operational & Information Sciences** Web page [19], includes the following departments:

1. Computer Sciences Department
2. Defense Analysis Department
3. Information Sciences Department
4. Operations Research Department

- **School of International Graduate Studies** Web page [20], operates multiple centers, including:

1. National Security Affairs Academic Program
2. Defense Resource Management Institute
3. Center for Contemporary Conflict
4. Center for Civil Military Relations Web page [21]
5. Center for Stabilization Reconstruction and Studies Web page [22]
6. Leadership Development and Education for Sustained Peace Web page [23]
7. International Defense and Acquisition Resource Management Web page [24]
8. Center for Homeland Defense and Security Web page [25]
9. International Graduate Program Office
10. Program for Culture & Conflict Studies Web page [26]

- **Center for Homeland Defense & Security**

NPS also operates an active Distributed Learning Program and Executive Education Programs for US warfighters and Civilian Government employees.

# History

On 9 June 1909, Secretary of the Navy George von L. Meyer signed General Order No. 27, establishing a school of marine engineering at Annapolis, Maryland.

On 31 October 1912, Meyer signed Navy General Order No. 233, which renamed the school the **Postgraduate Department of the United States Naval Academy**. The order established courses of study in ordnance and gunnery, electrical engineering, radio telegraphy, naval construction, and civil engineering as well as continuing the original program in marine engineering.

During World War II, Fleet Admiral Ernest King, chief of naval operations and commander-in-chief of both the Atlantic and Pacific fleets, established a commission to review the role of graduate education in the Navy. In 1945, Congress passed legislation to make the school a fully accredited, degree-granting graduate institution. Two years later, Congress adopted legislation authorizing the purchase of an independent campus for the school.

Herrmann Hall

A post-war review team, which had examined 25 sites nationwide, had recommended the old Hotel Del Monte in Monterey as a new home for the Postgraduate School. Negotiations with the Del Monte Properties Company led to the purchase of the hotel and 627 acres (2.5 km²) of surrounding land for $2.13 million.

In December 1951, the Postgraduate School moved across the nation, establishing its current campus in Monterey. Today, the school has over 40 programs of study including highly regarded M.S and PhD programs in electrical and computer engineering (NRC Ranking 68,[27] [28]), mechanical and astronautical engineering (NRC Ranking 30[29]), systems engineering, space systems and satellite engineering, physics, oceanography (NRC Ranking 22[30]), meteorology, applied mathematics,[31] computer science (NRC Ranking 83[32]), operations research, business and public policy (AACSB and NASPAA accredited, US News ranking 45[33]), international relations, and other disciplines, all with an emphasis on military applications. The Space Systems Academic Group of NPS has graduated thirty-three astronauts, more than any other graduate school in the country.[34] [35] NPS is home to the Center for Information Systems Security Studies and Research (CISR)[36] and the Center for Homeland Defense and Security (CHDS).[37] CISR is America's foremost center for defense-related research and education in Information Assurance (IA), Inherently Trustworthy Systems (ITC), and defensive information warfare; and CHDS provides the first homeland security master's degree in the United States.

# See also

- America's Army, a training video game developed at the MOVES Institute [38] at NPS
- Fleet Numerical Meteorology and Oceanography Center
- Richard Hamming
- Naval Postgraduate School's Center for Asymmetric Warfare (CAW)
- Official NPS Academic Calendar [39]
- Centre d'Etudes Diplomatiques et Stratégiques

# References

[1] As of 30 June 2009. "U.S. and Canadian Institutions Listed by Fiscal Year 2009 Endowment Market Value and Percentage Change in Endowment Market Value from FY 2008 to FY 2009" (http://www.nacubo.org/Documents/research/2009_NCSE_Public_Tables_Endowment_Market_Values.pdf) (PDF). *2009 NACUBO-Commonfund Study of Endowments*. National Association of College and University Business Officers. . Retrieved 2 February 2010.

[2] http://www.nps.edu/Administration/PresidentBio.html

[3] http://www.nps.edu/

[4] Research Associateship Programs (http://sites.nationalacademies.org/pga/rap/). Sites.nationalacademies.org. Retrieved on 17 October 2011.

[5] http://www.nps.edu/gsbpp

[6] http://www.nps.edu/Academics/GSEAS/index.html

[7] http://www.nps.edu/Academics/GSEAS/AppliedMath/index.html

[8] http://www.nps.edu/Academics/GSEAS/ECE/index.html

[9] http://www.nps.edu/Academics/GSEAS/MAE/

[10] http://www.nps.edu/Academics/GSEAS/Meteorology/index.html

[11] http://www.nps.edu/Academics/GSEAS/Oceanography/index.html

[12] http://www.nps.edu/Academics/GSEAS/Physics/index.html

[13] http://www.nps.edu/Academics/GSEAS/se/index.html

[14] http://www.nps.edu/Academics/GSEAS/SpaceSystems/index.html

[15] http://www.nps.edu/Academics/GSEAS/Navigation/Institutes.html

[16] http://www.nps.edu/Academics/GSEAS/usw/index.html

[17] http://www.nps.edu/RSC

[18] http://www.aa.nps.navy.mil/~mromano/SRL_public.htm

[19] http://www.nps.edu/Academics/Schools/GSOIS/index.html

[20] http://www.nps.edu/Academics/Schools/SIGS/index.html

[21] http://www.ccmr.org/public/home.cfm

[22] http://www.csrs-nps.org/logistica/public/home.cfm

[23] http://www.ldesp.org/public/home.cfm

[24] http://www.nps.edu/IDARM/

[25] http://www.chds.us/

[26] http://www.nps.edu/programs/ccs/index.html

[27] NRC Rankings in Each of 41 Areas (http://www.stat.tamu.edu/~jnewton/nrc_rankings/nrc41.html#area23). Stat.tamu.edu. Retrieved on 17 October 2011.

[28] Electrical & Computer Engineering Rankings (http://www.greguide.com/elecs.html). GRE Guide. Retrieved on 17 October 2011.

[29] NRC Rankings in Each of 41 Areas (http://www.stat.tamu.edu/~jnewton/nrc_rankings/nrc41.html#area19). Stat.tamu.edu. Retrieved on 17 October 2011.

[30] NRC Rankings in Each of 41 Areas (http://www.stat.tamu.edu/~jnewton/nrc_rankings/nrc41.html#area32). Stat.tamu.edu. Retrieved on 17 October 2011.

[31] Naval Postgraduate School – Applied Math (http://www.nps.edu/Academics/Schools/GSEAS/Departments/AppliedMath/index.html). Nps.edu (13 May 2011). Retrieved on 17 October 2011.

[32] NRC Rankings in Each of 41 Areas (http://www.stat.tamu.edu/~jnewton/nrc_rankings/nrc41.html#area29). Stat.tamu.edu. Retrieved on 17 October 2011.

[33] Best Graduate Schools | Top Graduate Programs | US News Education (http://grad-schools.usnews.rankingsandreviews.com/grad/public-affairs.html). Grad-schools.usnews.rankingsandreviews.com. Retrieved on 17 October 2011.

[34] http://www.npsfoundation.org/news.php

[35] http://www.nps.edu/Academics/GSEAS/SpaceSystems/PDF/NPS_Astronauts.pdf

[36] http://cisr.nps.edu/

[37] Center for Homeland Defense & Security (http://www.chds.us/). Chds.us. Retrieved on 17 October 2011.

[38] http://www.movesinstitute.org/

[39] http://www.nps.edu/Academics/Admissions/ImportantDates/Calendar.html

## External links

- Naval Postgraduate School (http://www.nps.edu/)

# National_Information_Exchange_Model

The **National Information Exchange Model** (**NIEM**, pronounced as 'Neam' similar to 'Team') is an XML-based information exchange framework from the United States. NIEM represents a collaborative partnership of agencies and organizations across all levels of government (federal, state, tribal, and local) and with private industry. The purpose of this partnership is to effectively and efficiently share critical information at key decision points throughout the whole of the justice, public safety, emergency and disaster management, intelligence, and homeland security enterprise. NIEM is designed to develop, disseminate, and support enterprise-wide information exchange standards and processes that will enable jurisdictions to automate information sharing.

NIEM is an outgrowth of the United States Department of Justice's Global Justice XML Data Model (GJXDM) project. NIEM is now being expanded to include other federal and state agencies such as the Office of the Director of National Intelligence, Federal Bureau of Investigation, Texas, Florida, New York, Pennsylvania, and others.

## Introduction

NIEM is not a software program, database, network, or computer system. NIEM is designed to facilitate the creation of automated enterprise-wide information exchanges which can be uniformly developed, centrally maintained, quickly identified and discovered, and efficiently reused. The result is more efficient and expansive information sharing between agencies and jurisdictions; more cost-effective development and deployment of information systems; improved operations; better quality decision making as a result of more timely, accurate, and complete information; and, as a consequence, enhanced public safety and homeland security.

## NIEM key concepts

The following key concepts are essential to understanding the purpose, architecture, processes, and other capabilities of NIEM, as well as to establish a common knowledge base with which to develop the ability to use NIEM effectively.

**Data Components.** The fundamental building block of NIEM is the data component. Data components are the basic business data elements that represent real-world objects and concepts. Information exchanged between agencies can be broken down into individual components – for example, information about people, places, material things, and events. Components that are frequently and uniformly used in practice are specified in NIEM and can then be reused by practitioners for information exchanges, regardless of the nature of their business or the operational context of their exchanges, provided they are semantically consistent.

**Information Exchange Package Documentation.** The information that is commonly or universally exchanged between participating domains can be organized into *information exchange packages* (IEPs) in the form of XML Schemas. An example of this collection of information is data associated with an arrest. The data to be exchanged includes not only descriptive and personal identification data regarding the individual arrested (i.e., the person component described above) but also information about the person's alleged offense, the location of the offense, the arresting officer, etc. The IEP represents a set of data that is actually transmitted between agencies for a specific business purpose (e.g., initiating a charging document by the local prosecutor). It includes the actual XML instance that delivers the payload or information. Additional information regarding this specific exchange can be further documented in the form of an *information exchange package documentation* (IEPD), which also contains data describing the structure, content, and other artifacts of the information exchange. An IEPD supports a specific set of business requirements in an operational setting.

**NIEM Core.** Data components within an information exchange that are universally shared and understood among all (or almost all) domains are identified as universal components (e.g., person, address, and organization). To become a universal component, consensus by all domains is needed on the semantics and structure of the component. The set of NIEM universal components is stable (once established) and relatively small.

**Domains.** For purposes of NIEM, a domain refers to a business enterprise broadly reflecting the agencies, units of government, operational functions, services, and information systems which are organized or affiliated to meet common objectives. NIEM domains are organized to facilitate governance, and each has some measure of persistency. Each domain traditionally includes a cohesive group of data stewards who are subject matter experts (SMEs), have some level of authority within the domains they represent, and participate in the processes related to harmonizing conflicts and resolving data component ambiguities.

**Communities of Interest.** Communities of interest (COIs) are collaborative groups of users who exchange information in pursuit of shared goals, interests, missions, or business processes and who therefore must have a shared vocabulary for the information they exchange. COIs reuse data components and artifacts found in NIEM to document their information exchanges. One or more COIs can coordinate to develop new domain content as they identify gaps in the data components needed for documenting information exchanges.

**NIEM Conformance.** There are NIEM conformance rules that serve as guidelines for agencies utilizing NIEM to implement their information sharing exchanges. Grantees developing inter-agency XML-based exchanges must comply with the special condition language contained in the grant, and follow the associated NIEM implementation guidelines.

# Organizational support

## NIEM Program Management Office

The NIEM Program Management Office (PMO) operates to:

- Bring stakeholders, agencies, and the domains and COIs that they represent together to identify information sharing requirements in daily operational and emergency situations;
- Develop information sharing standards, a common lexicon, and an online repository of information exchange package documentation and data components that support information sharing;
- Provide technical tools, processes, and methodologies to support the analysis, development, discovery, dissemination, and reuse of exchange standards and documents; and
- Provide training, technical assistance, communication, outreach, and implementation support services for NIEM-based information sharing.

## Training and other technical resources

NIEM is a continually evolving program, and new agencies and COIs are joining the effort all the time. As new stakeholders come on board, they need to receive information to gain understanding and knowledge of the core capabilities of NIEM and how to engage in NIE information exchanges. NIEM.gov provides training materials, such as briefings and process-related documentation, as well as other resources, such as the National Information Sharing Standards Help Desk and Knowledge Base [1]. Training provides the knowledge and know-how stakeholders need to use the tools and other capabilities provided by NIEM. NIEM tools and training opportunities are further described below. Other training materials, such as executive briefings, marketing material, and briefings for conferences and workshops, are offered from time to time and are tailored depending on the audience.

## NIEM.gov website

The NIEM Web site [2] serves as a primary means by which NIEM can provide the latest documentation and downloads to those interested in NIEM. It also serves as a starting point for those wishing to contact NIEM staff with questions, support, and information requests. As related projects, tools, and support resources develop around NIEM, the Web site will expand as the hub for these supplemental resources.

# Technical standards

NIEM adopts standard XML Schema constructs and methods, such as roles, associations, and augmentation from industry standards, such as the World Wide Web Consortium (W3C) XML Schema language.

## NIEM schemas

The NIEM reference schemas are a set of interrelated schemas that define NIEM data components. Each schema defines its own target namespace. Schemas in the reference set may import one another by namespace in order to use (or reuse) components they define. In general, domain reference schemas import schemas from the Core. The NIEM reference schema set represents the full set of data components in NIEM.

The following kinds of XML schemas are associated with the NIEM architecture:

- **NIEM reference schemas:** Schemas containing content created or approved by the NIEM steering committees are periodically released in schema distributions.
- **Subset Schema:** a NIEM-conformant schema, containing only the parts of the reference schemas needed to support a particular exchange.
- **Support schemas:** NIEM includes three special schemas, appinfo, structures and proxy, for annotating and structuring NIEM-conformant schemas.
- **Extension Schema:** a NIEM-conformant schema which adds domain- or application-specific content to the base NIEM model.
- **Exchange Schema:** a NIEM-conformant schema which specifies a document in a particular exchange.
- **Constraint Schema:** a NIEM-conformant schema which adds additional constraints to NIEM-conformant instances, but which is assumed to validate in concert with existing NIEM-conformant or subset schemas. A constraint schema need not validate constraints that are applied by other schemas.
- **Codelist Schemas:** a NIEM-conformant schema which provides a list of acceptable values that a data element will be constrained to.

The only mandatory schemas for validation are the NIEM reference schemas or a correct subset, however the IEPD specification requires that an IEPD include an exchange schema (along with the reference schemas or subsets) to be considered a complete IEPD. The NIEM schemas may import additional schemas, such as code table schemas, as needed. An optional extension schema may be used to add extended types and properties for components not contained in NIEM, but which are needed for the exchange.

## NIEM Naming and Design Rules (NDR)

The naming and design rules for NIEM are documented in the NIEM NDR [3], which specifies the data model, XML components, and XML data for use with NIEM and provides a basis for NIEM conformance. The current version is NDR v1.3, which was released on 2008-10-31.

NIEM is based on several concepts from the International Organisation for Standardisation (ISO) 11179, which provides guidelines for the naming and definition of data elements, as well as information about the metadata captured about data elements. Part 5 of the ISO 11179 standard [4] establishes a methodology for naming items in data dictionaries.

The ISO 11179-based NIEM NDR naming convention uses object class, property, and representation terms to constitute a multiple-part name as shown in the figure below:

**Object Class Term:** Represents the object to which the property is applicable. In NIEM, we interpret that object to be the real-world object. (An object class refers to a group of objects that share the same attributes, operations, methods, relationships, and semantics.)

**Property Term:** Identifies the property that the data element represents (e.g., last name, expiration date, height, total).

**Representation Term:** Describes the form of the data represented. This term is taken from a list of electronic business XML (ebXML) representation terms, including amount, code, date, time, graphic, identifier, indicator, measure, name, percent, picture, quantity, rate, time, and numeric.

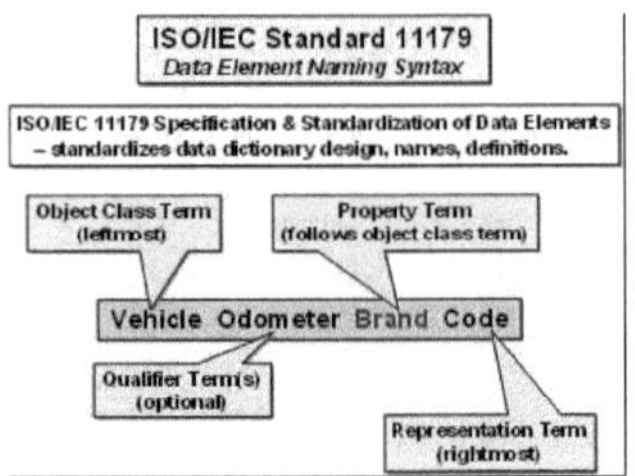


Example of an ISO standard data element name

**Qualifier Term:** The object class and property terms can have qualifiers; i.e., a word or words that help define and differentiate the element name.

## NIEM modeling and schema concepts

The NIEM technical modeling and schema concepts and mechanisms which support building new data components that meet specific requirements and reusing existing NIEM data components are briefly described below. More detail can be found in the NIEM User Guide and the NIEM NDR.

### Data elements, classes, types, and properties

The NIEM data model uses concepts originating from object-oriented programming (OOP). OOP defines a class as a specific entity in the data model, which may represent a real-world object but may also represent any conceptual object, such as relationships and messages. An object's properties are said to describe the object. When the NIEM XML Schemas are generated from the NIEM data model, data model classes are represented as XML Schema types, and data model properties are represented as XML elements and attributes.

### Extension techniques

There are two approaches for extending the NIEM data model for use in information exchange schemas and documents.

- Creating new NIEM types to represent new concepts
- Adding new data to existing NIEM types, to extend existing concepts

### Specialization with inheritance

Specialization is used when a base object class (type) contains or can be subcategorized into a more specific subclass. When this can be done, the subclass derived from the base class inherits the properties of the more general base or parent class. This mechanism is used to share or reuse properties between the general data component and its specialization. For example, a vehicle type (or class) is identified as a data component with properties of vehicle identification number (VIN), make, and model. Truck type (or class) is a specialization of vehicle and thus inherits the vehicle's properties but also has its own characteristic properties, such as truck bed length. Specialization is time independent and is generally used only when the base class and subclass always exist.

**Roles**

A role is a special type which represents a particular function, purpose, context, or activity for an entity. Roles are generally time dependent and, therefore, temporary. A new type can be created for a role when the role has specific data associated with it and its own life cycle. A role type has a property, RoleOf, which indicates what object is assuming this role. A single entity may assume multiple roles. For example, many different entities may assume the role of a weapon. Therefore, if a vehicle is used as a weapon (to attempt to injure or kill a person), then an instance of WeaponType would contain the property, RoleOf, which references the vehicle instance used as the weapon. The WeaponType (the role) might also contain properties that describe the persons and activities involved, dates and times of involvement, and how the entity was used as a weapon.

**Associations**

An association type is an object that represents a relationship between data components. For example, two PersonType instances, Abigail and Bob, could be referenced by a MarriageAssociationType to represent the fact they are married. The MarriageAssociationType could contain its own properties, such as date of marriage, number of children, date of divorce, death of one spouse, etc.

**Augmentation**

Augmentation of a NIEM data type allows the addition of domain- or model-specific information to the concept embodied in the NIEM type, without creating a new NIEM type. It would be impractical and unwieldy to include all possible domain model-specific properties in NIEM Core schemas for general use. Instead, domain modelers need to be able define data for their use, independently from common definitions. Furthermore, that data needs to be applicable to the NIEM data object itself, and reusable in multiple exchanges. The augmentation approach built into NIEM utilizes XML Schema constructs to reuse the existing XML schema representations for the data model, by allowing them to be augmented with the new information.

**Element substitution**

NIEM uses several techniques from XML Schema to allow as-needed element substitutions for pre-existing NIEM properties and into pre-existing NIEM types. Element substitution techniques allow the substitution of new XML Schema elements, representing derived NIEM properties that can be used where the parent properties are expected.

There are three XML Schema techniques that support the NIEM use of element substitutions:

- use of substitution groups
- creation of abstract, type-less elements, and
- use of abstract elements in reference schemas.

**Adapting external standards**

In addition to adding new NIEM types and properties to NIEM, it is possible to adapt existing external (non-NIEM) namespaces for use in the NIEM framework. This allows the use of external standards within NIEM IEPDs, without requiring that the external standards themselves be NIEM-conformant. The intent here is to allow use of external standard components exactly as they were defined.

**Metadata**

Metadata, or data about data, defines information that supports the actual content of XML instances. The metadata feature provides a mechanism for attaching structured properties that describe the pedigree or source (when reported, who reported, how reliable, etc.) of instance data to any data component of the model (type or object, property, association, role, or augmentation) in any namespace. It allows sets of metadata to be extended with additional properties for local requirements and enables metadata properties to be repeated.

### EIEM dictionary concepts

NIEM has introduced the concept of Enterprise Information Exchange Model (EIEM) dictionaries to allow NIEM implementers to position local collections of components specific to their own enterprise. Typically these may be drawn from an Enterprise Data Model (EDM) and then exported and refactored as XML components that conform to the NIEM NDR. See Tools section below for information on creating EIEM dictionaries.

# Tools

NIEM provides a reference set of tools [5] freely available with each NIEM release. The tools implement all of the structural and content features of the release, including the NIEM NDR. NIEM's well-defined interfaces and output products also support the development of independent third-party tools. Example supporting third party tools are listed below.

### NIEM XML data dictionary spreadsheet

The NIEM XML data dictionary spreadsheet [6] is a tangible representation of the entire NIEM data dictionary. It includes all of the element names that are organized hierarchically under core data components (person, property, organization, etc.) with hyperlinks to related elements. This spreadsheet also provides information on the type of data being represented (date, integer, string, etc.) and a precise, context-rich definition of each dictionary component.

### Information exchanges mapping tool

The Information Exchanges Mapping Tool [7] allows the user to specify metadata and upload XMI domain models associated with NIEM IEPDs, map components within domain models to NIEM components, and generate artifacts based on mappings, including mapping reports, wantlist, exchange schemas, extension schemas, and subset schemas.

### Schema Subset Generation Tool

The Schema Subset Generation Tool [8] (SSGT) enables users to search through the NIEM data model and build a NIEM subset. The NIEM data model covers several domains and typically not all of the data model is usable in an exchange. It is useful to make a schema subset of NIEM components to use in an exchange. It helps to limit the scope of developing an IEPD and can be built to the specific requirements of an exchange. With this tool users can:

- Search the data model from the Search Page.
- Navigate through the data model.
- Download already generated subsets from each domain.
- Build a schema subset containing the components required by their exchange.
- Save a list of components required for a subset.
- Upload a list of requested components to continue to edit it.
- Download a schema subset based on a list of required components.
- Create IEPD with current subset.
- Change the NIEM release used for building a schema subset.

### IEPD tool

The IEPD tool [9] enables the user to upload or enter the artifacts required for an IEPD (schemas, documentation, and metadata) and assembles into a package according to the IEPD specification. It can also validate that minimum artifacts and metadata are present. The user creates an account and is granted a work space ("My IEPDs"). Inside this work space, the user can upload the artifacts to construct any number of IEPDs (complete or partial); share them with other account holders; or search, discover, and download IEPDs that other account holders have marked for sharing.

A Model Package Description Specification [10] specifies the artifacts to be included in an IEPD or other Information Exchange Model (IEM).

Additionally see Third Party NIEM tools section below for IEPD tools that can automate much of the IEPD artifact generation. 3rd Party IEPD tool support includes automatic generation of NIEM cross-reference, wantlist.xml, exchange and subset schema, XML examples, rules documentation and NDR evaluation.

IEPDs which have been published to the IEPD Clearinghouse [11] are available for reuse by other organizations.

## Third Party NIEM development tools

The Wayfarer tool provides an alternative to the SSGT for designers to select existing components from the NIEM dictionary and assemble want lists for use in NIEM subset schema generation. Wayfarer [12]

The CAM (Content Assembly Mechanism) toolkit supports end to end development of IEPDs from inception to delivery of completed XSD schema, NDR evaluation, example XML test cases and business rule documentation tools. Also creation of EIEM dictionaries is supported and use of drag and drop visual designer editing with dictionary component collections. It is available as open source through the CAM processor on Sourceforge [13].

The toolkit is an implementation of the OASIS CAM v1.1 standard. The tools provide also support development of NIEM domain dictionaries and currently includes the LEXS 3.1.4 release dictionary along with local copies of NIEM 2.0 and NIEM 2.1 dictionaries in XML available here as spreadsheet [14]. The toolkit also supports importing enterprise data models, applying NDR checks and spelling and renaming automation. An introduction to the concepts of using the NIEM tools in CAM to develop NIEM IEPDs through either dictionaries and blueprints, or by ingesting existing XSD schema is available at the OASIS CAM TC documents website [15].

# NIEM status

As of October 2009, the current version is NIEM 2.1. It was released on September 28, 2009 and includes a number of enhancements:[16]

- Three new domains—Maritime; Family Services; and Chemical, Biological, Radiological, Nuclear (CBRN)
- Updates to the Justice, Infrastructure Protection, and Emergency Management domains
- Harmonization to reduce overlapping and duplicate data elements between domains
- Completion of plain-English definitions for all components
- 35% more content than NIEM 2.0

## Release history

- NIEM 2.1 Production Release – September 28, 2009
- NIEM 2.1 Release Candidate 1 – September 1, 2009
- NIEM 2.1 Beta 1 – July 29, 2009
- NIEM 2.0 Production Release – July 31, 2007
- NIEM 2.0 Release Candidate 2 – June 2007
- NIEM 1.0 Production Release – November 1, 2006
- NIEM 1.0 Release Candidate 1 – September 30, 2006
- NIEM 1.0 Beta 3 – September 11, 2006
- NIEM 1.0 Beta 2 – August 8, 2006
- NIEM 1.0 Beta 1 – June 30, 2006
- NIEM 0.3 – April 12, 2006
- NIEM 0.2.1 – February 24, 2006
- NIEM 0.2 – December 23, 2005
- NIEM 0.1 – October 11, 2005

## See also

- Rules for NIEM Conformance
- Global Justice XML Data Model (GJXDM)
- ISO/IEC 11179
- Metadata publishing
- Metadata registry
- Universal Core (UCore)

## References


[1] http://it.ojp.gov/NISS/helpdesk/

[2] http://www.niem.gov

[3] https://www.niem.gov/documentsdb/Documents/Technical/NIEM-NDR-1-3.pdf

[4] http://standards.iso.org/ittf/PubliclyAvailableStandards/c035347_ISO_IEC_11179-5_2005(E).zip

[5] http://tools.niem.gov/

[6] http://release.niem.gov/niem/2.1/niem-2.1.xls

[7] http://tools.niem.gov/niemtools/mapping/index.iepd

[8] http://tools.niem.gov/niemtools/ssgt/index.iepd

[9] http://tools.niem.gov/niemtools/iepdt/index.iepd

[10] http://reference.niem.gov/niem/specification/model-package-description/1.0/model-package-description-1.0.pdf

[11] http://it.ojp.gov/iepd/

[12] http://www.ncsconline.org/niemwayfarer/

[13] http://www.cameditor.org

[14] http://www.oasis-open.org/committees/document.php?document_id=36738

[15] http://www.oasis-open.org/committees/download.php/36147/CAM%20Exchange%20Content%20Assembly%20Blueprints.pdf

[16] "NIEM Newsletter" (http://www.askniem.org/newsletter200907.php). niem.gov. July 2009. . Retrieved 2011-09-01.


## External links

- The official NIEM.gov website (http://www.niem.gov)
- Justice Information Exchange Model (JIEM) Tool (http://it.ojp.gov/default.aspx?area=nationalInitiatives&
page=1110)

# Association_for_the_Advancement_of_Artificial_Intelli

| Association for the Advancement of Artificial Intelligence | |
|---|---|
| Formation | 1979 |
| Headquarters | Menlo Park, California |
| President | Henry Kautz |
| Website | www.aaai.org [1] |

The **Association for the Advancement of Artificial Intelligence** or **AAAI** is an international, nonprofit, scientific society devoted to advancing the scientific understanding of the mechanisms underlying thought and intelligent behavior and their embodiment in machines. AAAI also aims to increase public understanding of artificial intelligence (AI), improve the teaching and training of AI practitioners, and provide guidance for research planners and funders concerning the importance and potential of current AI developments and future directions.

## History

The organization was founded in 1979 under the name "**American Association for Artificial Intelligence**" and changed its name in 2007 to "Association for the Advancement of Artificial Intelligence". It has in excess of 6,000 members worldwide. In its early history, the organization was presided over by notable figures in computer science such as Allen Newell, Edward Feigenbaum, Marvin Minsky and John McCarthy. The previous president is Eric Horvitz, the president is Henry Kautz, and the president elect is Manuela Veloso.[2]

## Activities

The AAAI provides many services to the Artificial Intelligence community. The AAAI sponsors many conferences and symposia each year as well as providing support to 14 journals in the field of artificial intelligence. The AAAI also established the "AAAI Press" in association with the MIT Press in 1979 to produce books of relevance to artificial intelligence research. Additionally, the AAAI produces a quarterly publication, *AI Magazine*, which is written in such a way that it allows researchers to broaden the scope of their knowledge beyond their sub-fields. This magazine was first published in 1980.

AAAI organises the "AAAI Conference on Artificial Intelligence",[3] which is considered to be one of the top conferences in the field of artificial intelligence.[4] [5] Every other year, AAAI works with other AI organizations worldwide to put together the International Joint Conference on Artificial Intelligence (IJCAI).

## See also

- Fellows of the American Association for Artificial Intelligence
- List of artificial intelligence conferences

## References

[1] http://www.aaai.org/
[2] "AAAI Officials" (http://www.aaai.org/Organization/officers.php). . Retrieved 2011-03-03.
[3] "AAAI Conference on Artificial Intelligence" (http://www.aaai.org/Conferences/AAAI/aaai.php). . Retrieved 2009-10-16.
[4] "2007 Australian Ranking of ICT Conferences" (http://www.core.edu.au/rankings/Conference Ranking Main.html). . Retrieved 2009-10-16. Tier A+.
[5] "Top-ranked Conferences in "Artificial Intelligence"" (http://libra.msra.cn/CSDirectory/conf_category_5.htm). *Microsoft Academic Search*. . Retrieved 2009-10-16. Rank 2.

## External links

- AAAI.org (http://www.aaai.org/), AAAI official website

# Article Sources and Contributors

**Rick_Hayes-Roth**  *Source*: http://en.wikipedia.org/w/index.php?title=Rick_Hayes-Roth  *Contributors*: Adrignola, AllyD, CRKingston, CentralError, CommonsDelinker, D6, DGG, Daniel J. Leivick, JLaTondre, Jamestown, Jwillbur, Nhayesroth, PaulHanson, RJBurkhart3, Ryandake, Tassedethe, W Nowicki, 16 anonymous edits

**Chief_technology_officer**  *Source*: http://en.wikipedia.org/w/index.php?title=Chief_technology_officer  *Contributors*: Addaline, Alerante, Alexf, Amikake3, Anlace, Arcadie, Arnoldgibson, Ary29, Astatine-210, Bowman, Brian Huffman, BryanD, Chris the speller, CloudNine, Cybercobra, Danlev, David Latapie, Dennos, Dub617, Epheterson, Ettrig, Ewlyahoocom, GoldenGoose100, Ground Zero, Hristodulo, I am neuron, IHTFP, JTN, Jeromeflipo, Jluismarin, Krazymike, Kuru, L337 kybldmstr, Lcapitulino, Leolaursen, Leuko, LiDaobing, LuisAugustoPeña, MMuzammils, Mediathink, Meelar, Mkns, Nat Krause, Netoholic, Neutrality, Nickshanks, Odie5533, Ohnoitsjamie, OwenX, Padams, Phm002028, Pitoutom, Pomte, Postcard Cathy, Pravin.taskseveryday, Pwpett, RP459, Reach Out to the Truth, Richard@lbrc.org, Rob Kennedy, Roger.smith, Ronhjones, Ronz, Rsgdodge, Rummey, Seth Nimbosa, Smaines, Spafinder, Srbauer, Stan Shebs, Stephenb, Tellmewhy1, Template namespace initialisation script, Tomjenkins52, Torchy 2008, W E Hill, Wiki3 1415, Wikix, Zelig123456, 114 anonymous edits

**Hewlett-Packard**  *Source*: http://en.wikipedia.org/w/index.php?title=Hewlett-Packard  *Contributors*: (jarbarf), -Majestic-, 123abcwiki, 13139913, 16@r, 1ForTheMoney, 1wax, 213.253.39.xxx, 7severn7, A Man In Black, A.arvind.arasu, ARC Gritt, ARUNKUMAR P.R, AST3, AThing, Aang, Abhimp, AbsolutDan, Abtract, Academic Challenger, Addshore, Adlkjf, Admrboltz, Adraeus, Adrian-polglase, Aeons, Aerotheque, Aetylus, After Midnight, AgadaUrbanit, Ahoerstemeier, Ahpook, Aido2002, Airplaneman, Aizuku, Ajaxfan, Akshaypr, Alan Liefting, Alansohn, Alcuin, Aldie, Alec2710, Alfie66, Alison, Alison9, AlistairMcMillan, Allen3, Amcl, Amillar, Anaxial, Andros 1337, Andy.man1997, Anmol singh, Anole 418, Anon lynx, Antandrus, Antennaman, Aomarks, Apathy913, Appraiser, Aremith, Ari21, Arjuna, Arnoha, Artyomszeg, Arx Fortis, Asalado90, Asimkhan0001, Astor14, Astuishin, Atlant, Austin126, Awatt6, Axlrosen, Ayanchinov, B Touch, B4hand, B64, BD2412, BWCNY, Baccala, Bal3d, BalderV, Bancham, Banstaman, Banus, Bardya4, Barek, Baronnet, Bartfat, Baseball Bugs, Baylink, Bboyskidz, Bbpen, Beinsane, Belovedfreak, Bender235, Bentogoa, Bgpaulus, Bhilly, Bigfoot's Curse of the Wild, Bissinger, Bjbjk2, Bjbushpig, Black Falcon, Blaxthos, Bobjuch, Bollyjeff, Bonadea, Bongomatic, Bongwarrior, Boothy443, Bradv, Brawrg1, BrekekekexKoaxKoax, Brewcrewer, Bridgeplayer, Brigclark, BrokenSphere, BrotherFlounder, Brucedp, Brutaldeluxe, Bryan Derksen, Bt8257, Btornado, Buffs, Bugnot, Bull-Doser, Burgundavia, C628, CUBJONES83, CWenger, Cab88, Cactus2, Caknuck, Calbaer, CambridgeBayWeather, Cameron Scott, Canaima, CanisRufus, Carlossuarez46, Casieg, Cavinx, Cbmaster, Cc walsh, Cc68, Ccirulli, Chadlupkes, Chaitanya.lala, CherryTreeAmericans, Cheung1303, Chickyfuzz14, ChicosBailBonds, Chris the speller, Chris-Gonzales, Chrislk02, Chrisn4255, Ck lostsword, Cleared as filed, CliffC, Closedmouth, Cmichael, Colin Keigher, Colonies Chris, Common appeal, CommonsDelinker, Comphy3, ComputerVancouverite, ConcernedVancouverite, Conversion script, Coolcaesar, Cozy43, Cpqdon, Crabworld, Crazymonkey1123, Crazytales, Crocodile Punter, Cureden, CyclePat, Cziems, DIEXEL, DMG413, Da Joe, DaDrumBum, DaMenace123, DabMachine, Dabomb87, Daen, Dale Arnett, Damon Mah, DanTheMan702, Danallen46, Dannydream9999, Darkfred, Darkred, Dave Mott, DavidJackson, Davshul, Dawn Bard, Dawnseeker2000, Deanh, Deathawk, Deathforglory, Dedmond29, Dekisugi, Deryck Chan, DesuDesuDesuDesu3, Dewhastme, Dicklyon, DigitalMediaSage, Dillard421, Dipankan001, DirectEdge, Diyar se, DizzyITTech, Doczilla, Donfbreed, Donreed, DragonHawk, Dreadstar, Dream out loud, Drilnoth, Dungsff, Dzhim, Dzubint, EVula, Eagles247, Eastlaw, Ebyabe, EditorInTheRye, Edivorce, Eduardo Sellan III, Edward, Edwtie, ElliotThomas, Epbr123, Eric.d.dixon, Eric42, Error -128, Esanchez7587, Esoteric Rogue, Eurosong, Eustress, EvelinaB, Evice, EvocativeIntrigue, Evosoho, Evrik, Exit2DOS2000, Exploding Toenails, FAEP, FaheyUSMC, Fairlyoddparents1234, Falcon 94, Falcon8765, Fanjw007, Favonian, Ffokoob, Firsfron, FisherQueen, Flakeoff101, Flamurai, Flewis, Flyguy649, Fmiletic, Folajimi, Folksong, Fram, Franklinwangqiong, Frap, Fredrik, FreplySpang, Fudoreaper, Futureobservatory, Fuzzygenius, Galloping Moses, Gardar Rurak, Garglebutt, Gargouille 238, Gavin Wilson, Geertivp, Geniac, GeorgiKobilarov, Gettingtoit, Ghlinn, Gilliam, Glst2, Gnangarra, Gobonobo, Gogo Dodo, Golbez, GoldDragon, Goldfinger288, Gr1st, GraemeL, Graham87, Greenguy1090, Greenshed, GregorB, Gribeco, Gronky, Ground Zero, Grunt, Gsarwa, Guliolopez, Gump Stump, H0dd0ck, HP dv 1000, Hairy Dude, Hankyeol, Hao2lian, Happysailor, HaraldKoch, Haseo9999, HatlessAtlas, Hauser, Hcanon, Hdante, Headbomb, Hede2000, Henry W. Schmitt, HereToHelp, Hippasus, Hippo Potamus, Hoo man, Hooperbloob, Hpian, Hpmemproject, Hult041956, Hunter Kahn, Hydnjo, Hydrargyrum, Hydrogen Iodide, I Own Alienware, I5bala, Ian Wegg, IanGriffin, Idaltu, Illinois2011, Imgaril, In2thats12, Interlingua, Iohannes Animosus, Iquehd, Iridescent, Isnow, Ispy1981, Itsmejudith, J, J.delanoy, J.smith, JCDenton2052, JCRules, JCam, JGXenite, JLRedperson, JLaTondre, Jab843, Jacoplane, Jaizovic, Jalo, Jamcib, JamesBWatson, Jamesedwardlong, Jasenlee, JasonAQuest, Jay, Jboorman01, Jcheckler, Jeffq, Jensemann, Jerem43, Jeremy Visser, Jerryseinfeld, Jerrysmp, Jesper Gerved, Jezarnold, Jhessela, Jim Becker, Jim1138, JimmyjOHNS38, Jimzo, Jj137, Jjnguy, Jklme, Jmtaylor90, Jnk, JoanneB, Jodicy, JoeWiki, Joeschmoe321, John, John K, John254, JohnFromPinckney, JohnnyMrNinja, Jojhutton, JonHarder, Jonnytran, Joseph Solis in Australia, Jovianeye, Jpbrenna, Jpers36, Jplatt39, Jrockley, Jsayre64, Juan.forero22, Juhachi, Julia W, Junglecat, Jvandyke, Jvcdude, Jvlock, Jwojdylo, Jxl180, Jæs, KKvistad, KSweeley, Kaghup6, Kamix, Kappa, Karebear 1022, Kareeser, Karenreynolds, Kbdank71, Keesekuchen, Kelw, Keno, Kevndcks, Khalid Mahmood, Kierant, King of Hearts, Kiore, Kirils, Kitty31, Kkm010, Knowsetfree, Koman90, Kookykman, Kosunen, Kozuch, Kpjas, Krawi, Kristod, Kristof vt, Kubanczyk, Kubik 8344, Kuru, Kuthup, Kwiki, L'Aquatique, LA2, LG4761, Lagrange613, Lahhtims, Lanky, Laurusnobilis, Leranedo, Liam Braithwaite, Liangent, Lightmouse, LikeLakers2, LilHelpa, Lila Cheney 336, LittleWink, Locos epraix, Lordvolton, Lotje, Lowflyingowl, Luapnampahc, Luiseargote, Luisiana, Luna Santin, Lwalt, Lykovaa, M-hwang, M.Fin.User, M3lm4tt, M4gnum0n, MFfan310, MR.SHANDO, Mac John Concord, Macduff, Macpl, Magnus.de, Mairi, Malpass93, Managerarc, Mardus, Marek69, Markie111, Markpeak, Martarius, Martinlangley01, Master Deusoma, Master Jay, Match 467, Mathewd48, Mathwiz9, Matt Borak, Matthew Woodcraft, Mav, Mcginnly, MeekMark, Mehudson1, Mervyn, Mewtwowimmer, Mgd2010, Mhopeng, Michaeluram, Mifter, Mike Simons, Mikerooney, Minesweeper, Mirmo!, Miron82, Mjquinn id, Mjsabby, Mll1013, Mlpearc Public, Mlsquad, Mmm333k, MolotovH, More Coreyander, Moshe Constantine Hassan Al-Silverburg, MrChupon, MrCyber, MrMunky, MrSomeone, Mrath, Mrcook9, Mrpauliepaul1, Mrschimpf, Myscrnnm, Nabild, Nakon, Naniwako, NapoliRoma, Nasnema, NauarchLysander, NawlinWiki, Nazaregg, NeilN, Neilbeach, Neutrality, NewEnglandYankee, Nichalp, NickBush24, Nighthawkzx, Nishkid64, Nitinkillaepic, Nnatmc2007, No1lakersfan, Nono64, Nonzerobubble, Northamerica1000, Notedgrant, Nufy8, Nuno valente19, Nurg, OakleyCA, Octahedron80, Oda Mari, OhanaUnited, Ohconfucius, Ohnoitsjamie, Oknazevad, OlEnglish, Oldag07, Oli Filth, Olivier, Omologato, One, Oo64eva, Opelio, Orangemike, Orcaman, Oroso, Orz, Osama bin dipesh, Ottawahitech, OwenX, Oxymoron83, Ozguroot, P0lyglut, PacoRabolo, Pairadox, Pak21, Palmpilot, Pamri, Paraparamedic, Parhamr, Parthrana, Patrrickkk, Patstuart, Pearinc., Pearle, Pevernagie, Pgenie, PhilKnight, Philippe (WMF), Phlegat, Pinethicket, Pink Bull, Placeposition, Plasticup, PleaseStand, Ploca12, Pobrien, Pol099, Polluxian, Pomte, Printerdoc, Privatechef, Priyankadaga, Probity incarnate, Prolog, PubLife, Puredesi123456789, Quadell, QuantumCypher, Qwqwqw99, R. S. Shaw, RJHall, RTC, Rabhyanker, RadicalBender, RadioKirk, Raghavsethi, Raj alam01, Rama, RandomP, Rangoon11, Raysonho, Rbyrd8100, Rcawsey, Rdsmith4, Reach Out to the Truth, Reaper Eternal, RedHillian, Redeagle119, Rees11, Reginmund, Reisio, Renaissance Man, RepublicanJacobite, Retodon8, Rettetast, Rexdrums69, Rgb9000, Rhobite, Rhsatrhs, Ricardocolombia, Ricardocucuta, Rich Farmbrough, Richi, Ricksy, Ricky81682, Rilak, Rimau007, Rjwilmsi, Rklawton, Rob1974, Robguru, RockMFR, Roded86400, Roger Hui, Rohitbhaijain, RoyBoy, Rtcpenguin, RyanGerbil10, S51438, SAGNIPSAGNIP, SNIyer12, Saganaki-, Sahils1512, Sahrin, Salam32, Salamurai, Salmans801, SamJohnston, Samsara, SamuelRiv, Sander Säde, Sandstorm6299, Sardanaphalus, Sarranduin, Saugatadas1, Savoy rattler, Schmeitgeist, Scientizzle, Scrambler 321, Scriberius, Sealman, SeanMack, Seaphoto, Sen amitava, Seqsea, Sfahey, Shadowjams, Shady69, Shauni84, Shawnc, ShokuMasterLord, Sibi antony, SidP, Sietse Snel, Sigma 7, Siliconov, Sir Stanley, Skywolf, Smash, Snowynight, Snoyes, Soap, Softy, Solarisworld, Somebody in the WWW, Spangineer, Spearhead, SpiderJon, Spilla, Spimeco, SpuriousQ, Spykidz, Squash Racket, Squids and Chips, Stan Shebs, StaticGull, Stephend01, Stepheng3, SteveSims, Stevenmitchell, Straif, Styrofoam1994, Suater, Sunshine Warrior04, Superbeecat, SusanLesch, Svntnth, Syrthiss, THEunique, TMV943, TRIBESMAN, TShiozaki, TaerkastUA, Takuy, Tannin, Tanthalas39, TaraPan, Tascha96, Tassedethe, Tbhotch, Tbo 157, Technopat, Techtoine, Tedder, Teddy 80087, Tedp, Teh tennisman, The Anome, The Land of Smeg, The wub, The1McShane, TheProject, TheQuandry, Theda, Thegn, Thegreatglobetrotter, TheiPodKid, Themfromspace, Thendral Muthusami, Thepangelinanpost, Theropod-X, Thingg, Throup, Thumperward, Tiggerjay, Tim Chambers, Tim1357, Tinton5, Tkaizan, Tmuzzatti, Tom, Tonkie67, Torinir, Tourdeforcex, Toussaint, Tregoweth, Trekphiler, Trevor MacInnis, Trey Kinkead, Trey.reynolds, Trident13, Tripod86, Trusilver, Tygar, Typhoon, Uagehry456, UkPaolo, Ulric1313, Ump45silenced, Unconstructivemojoman, Urod, Utcursch, UtherSRG, Valfontis, Vancouverguy, Vanished user lkdfj39u3mfk4, Vchimpanzee, Vegaswikian, Veila, Velella, Venomm 0932, Vinayak.s, Vinoo202, Vipinhari, Vlad, Vlahd, Vology, Vqk5018, Vvn india, Warfvinge, Waycool27, Wefoij, Wernher, West.andrew.g, Weyes, Wgungfu, WhisperToMe, Wik, Wiki alf, Wiki13, Wikid77, Wikitawe, Winbuyer, Wireless Keyboard, Wmahan, Wocis, Wonderbiscuit, Woohookitty, Wootingfuner, Woz2, Wpc-01, WriterListener, Wtyler, X-Fi6, X1987x, X96vmn, XJamRastafire, Xaltotun, Ximaera, Xnatedawgx, Xp54321, Xtreme racer, Xvxonline17, Yatou9, Yellowjacket1, Yenom123, Youssefsan, Yoyoma223, ZacBowling, Zeamays, Zeartiste, Zelikazi, Zeppomedio, Zer0431, ZimZalaBim, Zippy, Zodon, Zoicon5, Zom 958, Zondor, Zooterkin, Zsinj, Zummis, Zzblue, ^demon, ~obsidian, Δ, סרה, רוּם, 1417 anonymous edits

**Edward_Feigenbaum**  *Source*: http://en.wikipedia.org/w/index.php?title=Edward_Feigenbaum  *Contributors*: 3omarz, A Kit, AdamSmithee, All Hallow's Wraith, Amillar, Andrei Stroe, Asiananimal, BenjaminTsai, CanisRufus, CharlesGillingham, D6, David Eppstein, David Gerard, Dmcguinness, GioCM, Gzornenplatz, Hike395, JMSwtlk, Janm67, Jayamohan, Joshua Andersen, KYPark, Kbdank71, Klemen Kocjancic, Koavf, Looxix, Marketdiamond, Masterpiece2000, Nima Baghaei, OwenX, Pgr94, RedWolf, Rich Farmbrough, Robert Merkel, SchreyP, Slo-mo, SpuriousQ, Tassedethe, Thom2729, ThreePD, Torla42, Trevj, Wikiwikiwikiwikiwiki, Wizardman, Zouxiaohui, 19 anonymous edits

**RAND_Corporation**  *Source*: http://en.wikipedia.org/w/index.php?title=RAND_Corporation  *Contributors*: 3mta3, A. J. Rizzo, Absolutely, Acedork87, AdRock, Addshore, Aegis Maelstrom, AgadaUrbanit, Akds, Alan Canon, Alan Liefting, Alansohn, Alexf, Alsadius, Anonyhole, Anonymousswiki, Apokrif, ArnoldReinhold, Atlantabravz, Auric04, Avaya1, Awotter, AxelBoldt, BBSR71, Bananafish, Barslori, Bdb484, Biruitorul, Bkonrad, BlaiseFEgan, Bleeter, Bless sins, Boscobiscotti, Boston, Branonm, Brighterorange, BrokenSegue, BurnDownBabylon, CLW, CMG, Captainktainer, Cbl62, Charaw, Charles Gaudette, Charles Matthews, Chrisboote, Clappingsimon, Claratee, Colonies Chris, Conversion script, CoolGuy, Crosbiesmith, Crucible31, Cutline, D6, DMCer, Dan Guan, Dantheman, Davis39, Dbarnes99, Dduff442, DerHexer, Doc Comic, DocWilson, Doom-chronicle, ENeville, Earthstar, Eastlaw, Ecleath, Ellywa, Elmindreda, Elonka, Erkan Yilmaz, Ewlyahoocom, Farhikht, Fastfission, Feezo, Felipe P, Fences and windows, Fnlayson, Friedo, Fritzpoll, GVP Webmaster, Garion96, GeraldH, Gerling, GraemeL, Graham87, Grandpafootsoldier, Gregbard, Guaka, Guy Harris, HGB, Harryboyles, Headbomb, HelgeStenstrom, Hellbus, Henrygb, Hibernian, HoboJones, Howardjp, Howrealisreal, Hpainter, Hydrargyrum, Ikip, Itaque422, JEB90, JHFTC, Jaganath, Jason Recliner, Esq., Jdabney, Jeff G., Jeph paul, Jeremymiles, Jfdwolff, Jivecat, Joelwhit, John, Johnpacklambert, Jonathan.s.kt, JonathanDP81, Jordanp, Joseph Solis in Australia, Journalist1983, Jpmayberry, Kasaalan, Kaysov, Kejoxen, Kingturtle, Koavf, Konrad West, Kross, Kurieeto, La goutte de pluie, Lapaz, Larklight, Lcleath, Levineps, Ligtvoet, Lingust, Lir, Liujiang, Logologist, Loren.wilton, Lyra9514, M3927, MARIOFREAK17, Maurice Carbonaro, Maury Markowitz, Mdd, Meelar, Mike1024, MikeEagling, Mikedelsol, Morning star, Mozzerati, Mxn, N328KF, NYScholar, Namesinger, Nat Krause, Neutralitydrive, Numbat, Nv8200p, Olivier, Ourai, Paul Richter, PaulHanson, Pearle, Phe, Phil Bastian, Phoebe13, Pinar, Pmedema, Prestonmcconkie, Publicus, QuackGuru, Quackslikeaduck, Quadell, Rama, Raul654, Rich Farmbrough, Richard Arthur Norton (1958- ), Richard L. Peterson, RichardVeryard, Rjhatl, Rjwilmsi, Robert Brockway, Robomanx, Rolypolyman, SDC, Saedon, SarahStierch, Sartoresartus, SchuminWeb, Sclm, Seano1, Sen dp, Shannondale, Sheeson, Shino Baku, Shirt58, Shizzy9989, Shootbamboo, Shortride, Sindujas, Snicholls, Splash, Squandermania, Squash Racket, Stevenmitchell, Str1977, Tabletop, Tarotcards, Teaforthetillerman,

Technopilgrim, Thaurisil, The wub, Three-quarter-ten, Thunder77, Timo Honkasalo, Tleong, TraumaPony, Trivialist, Una Smith, Vegaswikian, Vera Cruz, Vernon39, VoX, Warrenpe, Wencolberg, Wham Bam Rock II, Whbjr, WideArc, Wikishotaro, Wildcursive, Will Beback, Woohookitty, Wspencer11, Xtraeme, Yossarian4010, Zalethon, Zc Abc, Чрьный человек, 269 anonymous edits

**Blackboard_system** *Source*: http://en.wikipedia.org/w/index.php?title=Blackboard_system *Contributors*: Abto, Adorilson, Ajpeters, Alai, Bediako, Charles Matthews, Dancorkill, Enderminh, Fl, Fountainofignorance, Gomezfox, Gp5588, History2007, Hthth, Hydraton31, JMSwtlk, Joswig, JulesH, Landercorkill, Lengyeltom, Lotje, Lycurgus, Lysy, Pgan002, Remuel, Rpyle731, UkPaolo, Washi, Wolfc01, 34 anonymous edits

**Naval_Postgraduate_School** *Source*: http://en.wikipedia.org/w/index.php?title=Naval_Postgraduate_School *Contributors*: 2D, 72Dino, A2Kafir, Absolon, Aeh4543, Akradecki, Badbilltucker, Barticus88, Bobblewik, Bobcio, Cameronc, CanisRufus, Captain Cheeks, Chris the speller, Cisc0123, Cpastern, D6, Dholwell, Djharrity, Dlauri, DocWatson42, Docu, Eagle4000, Eaglearnn, Epolk, Evans1982, Fdacosta, Fernando S. Aldado, Hal99, Halmonster, HarryHenryGebel, Hawaiian717, Hmains, Hughey, Hvyhammer, JJL, Jamestown, Jericho48, Jllm06, John of Reading, Johnpacklambert, Jonathantreichel, Kafziel, Ke6jjj, LarryJeff, Looper5920, Maralia, Masonpatriot, Maximus Rex, Mean as custard, Mitamarine, Muj0, N5iln, Ndunruh, Nihil novi, Nobunaga24, Ohconfucius, Opsetc31, PaulHanson, Pecio2, RJBurkhart3, Rmhermen, Simsong, Squalk25, Stepheng3, TelecomNut, Timlevin, Tomcool, Uuuussseeeerrrnnnaaaammmmeeee, Welsh, XLerate, Xsmith, 59 anonymous edits

**National_Information_Exchange_Model** *Source*: http://en.wikipedia.org/w/index.php?title=National_Information_Exchange_Model *Contributors*: Barticus88, Bunnyhop11, ChemGardener, Dabystru, Dmccreary, Doug Bell, Drrwebber, Gaius Cornelius, Gregbard, Hulmem, ITBlair, Joinarnold, JonHarder, Jpbowen, Karada, Knowlengr, Mhaslip, Michael Hardy, Mohammadchoobin, Mrdvt92, NIEM Guy, Peter, RayGates, Rich Farmbrough, Stephenpace, 65 anonymous edits

**Association_for_the_Advancement_of_Artificial_Intelligence** *Source*: http://en.wikipedia.org/w/index.php?title=Association_for_the_Advancement_of_Artificial_Intelligence *Contributors*: AaronSloman, Aboutmovies, Andychun, Beefyt, Brambleclawx, Chaosdruid, CharlesGillingham, David Eppstein, Delirium, Disavian, Finin, Frank Shearar, Gioto, Infrogmation, Jpbowen, Laepdjek, Lotje, Lquilter, Michael Fourman, Miym, Quatloo, Raul654, Riwilmsi, Sam Hocevar, Scaife, Shadow Knight1234, SimonP, Sm8900, SocratesJedi, Tiaio, Walaaelki, Митя1991, بوعزی, 17 anonymous edits

# Image Sources, Licenses and Contributors

GNU Free Documentation License Version 1.2, November 2002 Copyright (C) 2000,2001,2002 Free Software Foundation, Inc. 59 Temple Place, Suite 330, Boston, MA 02111-1307 USA Everyone is permitted to copy and distribute verbatim copies of this license document, but changing it is not allowed.

0. PREAMBLE
The purpose of this License is to make a manual, textbook, or other functional and useful document "free" in the sense of freedom: to assure everyone the effective freedom to copy and redistribute it, with or without modifying it, either commercially or noncommercially. Secondarily, this License preserves for the author and publisher a way to get credit for their work, while not being considered responsible for modifications made by others. This License is a kind of "copyleft", which means that derivative works of the document must themselves be free in the same sense. It complements the GNU General Public License, which is a copyleft license designed for free software. We have designed this License in order to use it for manuals for free software, because free software needs free documentation: a free program should come with manuals providing the same freedoms that the software does. But this License is not limited to software manuals; it can be used for any textual work, regardless of subject matter or whether it is published as a printed book. We recommend this License principally for works whose purpose is instruction or reference.

1. APPLICABILITY AND DEFINITIONS
This License applies to any manual or other work, in any medium, that contains a notice placed by the copyright holder saying it can be distributed under the terms of this License. Such a notice grants a world-wide, royalty-free license, unlimited in duration, to use that work under the conditions stated herein. The "Document", below, refers to any such manual or work. Any member of the public is a licensee, and is addressed as "you". You accept the license if you copy, modify or distribute the work in a way requiring permission under copyright law. A "Modified Version" of the Document means any work containing the Document or a portion of it, either copied verbatim, or with modifications and/or translated into another language. A "Secondary Section" is a named appendix or a front-matter section of the Document that deals exclusively with the relationship of the publishers or authors of the Document to the Document's overall subject (or to related matters) and contains nothing that could fall directly within that overall subject. (Thus, if the Document is in part a textbook of mathematics, a Secondary Section may not explain any mathematics.) The relationship could be a matter of historical connection with the subject or with related matters, or of legal, commercial, philosophical, ethical or political position regarding them. The "Invariant Sections" are certain Secondary Sections whose titles are designated, as being those of Invariant Sections, in the notice that says that the Document is released under this License. If a section does not fit the above definition of Secondary then it is not allowed to be designated as Invariant. The Document may contain zero Invariant Sections. If the Document does not identify any Invariant Sections then there are none. The "Cover Texts" are certain short passages of text that are listed, as Front-Cover Texts or Back-Cover Texts, in the notice that says that the Document is released under this License. A Front-Cover Text may be at most 5 words, and a Back-Cover Text may be at most 25 words. A "Transparent" copy of the Document means a machine-readable copy, represented in a format whose specification is available to the general public, that is suitable for revising the document straightforwardly with generic text editors or (for images composed of pixels) generic paint programs or (for drawings) some widely available drawing editor, and that is suitable for input to text formatters or for automatic translation to a variety of formats suitable for input to text formatters. A copy made in an otherwise Transparent file format whose markup, or absence of markup, has been arranged to thwart or discourage subsequent modification by readers is not Transparent. An image format is not Transparent if used for any substantial amount of text. A copy that is not "Transparent" is called "Opaque". Examples of suitable formats for Transparent copies include plain ASCII without markup, Texinfo input format, LaTeX input format, SGML or XML using a publicly available DTD, and standard-conforming simple HTML, PostScript or PDF designed for human modification. Examples of transparent image formats include PNG, XCF and JPG. Opaque formats include proprietary formats that can be read and edited only by proprietary word processors, SGML or XML for which the DTD and/or processing tools are not generally available, and the machine-generated HTML, PostScript or PDF produced by some word processors for output purposes only. The "Title Page" means, for a printed book, the title page itself, plus such following pages as are needed to hold, legibly, the material this License requires to appear in the title page. For works in formats which do not have any title page as such, "Title Page" means the text near the most prominent appearance of the work's title, preceding the beginning of the body of the text. A section "Entitled XYZ" means a named subunit of the Document whose title either is precisely XYZ or contains XYZ in parentheses following text that translates XYZ in another language. (Here XYZ stands for a specific section name mentioned below, such as "Acknowledgements", "Dedications", "Endorsements", or "History".) To "Preserve the Title" of such a section when you modify the Document means that it remains a section "Entitled XYZ" according to this definition. The Document may include Warranty Disclaimers next to the notice which states that this License applies to the Document. These Warranty Disclaimers are considered to be included by reference in this License, but only as regards disclaiming warranties: any other implication that these Warranty Disclaimers may have is void and has no effect on the meaning of this License.

2. VERBATIM COPYING
You may copy and distribute the Document in any medium, either commercially or noncommercially, provided that this License, the copyright notices, and the license notice saying this License applies to the Document are reproduced in all copies, and that you add no other conditions whatsoever to those of this License. You may not use technical measures to obstruct or control the reading or further copying of the copies you make or distribute. However, you may accept compensation in exchange for copies. If you distribute a large enough number of copies you must also follow the conditions in section 3. You may also lend copies, under the same conditions stated above, and you may publicly display copies.

3. COPYING IN QUANTITY
If you publish printed copies (or copies in media that commonly have printed covers) of the Document, numbering more than 100, and the Document's license notice requires Cover Texts, you must enclose the copies in covers that carry, clearly and legibly, all these Cover Texts: Front-Cover Texts on the front cover, and Back-Cover Texts on the back cover. Both covers must also clearly and legibly identify you as the publisher of these copies. The front cover must present the full title with all words of the title equally prominent and visible. You may add other material on the covers in addition. Copying with changes limited to the covers, as long as they preserve the title of the Document and satisfy these conditions, can be treated as verbatim copying in other respects. If the required texts for either cover are too voluminous to fit legibly, you should put the first ones listed (as many as fit reasonably) on the actual cover, and continue the rest onto adjacent pages. If you publish or distribute Opaque copies of the Document numbering more than 100, you must either include a machine-readable Transparent copy along with each Opaque copy, or state in or with each Opaque copy a computer-network location from which the general network-using public has access to download using public-standard network protocols a complete Transparent copy of the Document, free of added material. If you use the latter option, you must take reasonably prudent steps, when you begin distribution of Opaque copies in quantity, to ensure that this Transparent copy will remain thus accessible at the stated location until at least one year after the last time you distribute an Opaque copy (directly or through your agents or retailers) of that edition to the public. It is requested, but not required, that you contact the authors of the Document well before redistributing any large number of copies, to give them a chance to provide you with an updated version of the Document.

4. MODIFICATIONS
You may copy and distribute a Modified Version of the Document under the conditions of sections 2 and 3 above, provided that you release the Modified Version under precisely this License, with the Modified Version filling the role of the Document, thus licensing distribution and modification of the Modified Version to whoever possesses a copy of it. In addition, you must do these things in the Modified Version: A. Use in the Title Page (and on the covers, if any) a title distinct from that of the Document, and from those of previous versions (which should, if there were any, be listed in the History section of the Document). You may use the same title as a previous version if the original publisher of that version gives permission. B. List on the Title Page, as authors, one or more persons or entities responsible for authorship of the modifications in the Modified Version, together with at least five of the principal authors of the Document (all of its principal authors, if it has fewer than five), unless they release you from this requirement. C. State on the Title page the name of the publisher of the Modified Version, as the publisher. D. Preserve all the copyright notices of the Document. E. Add an appropriate copyright notice for your modifications adjacent to the other copyright notices. F. Include, immediately after the copyright notices, a license notice giving the public permission to use the Modified Version under the terms of this License, in the form shown in the Addendum below. G. Preserve in that license notice the full lists of Invariant Sections and required Cover Texts given in the Document's license notice. H. Include an unaltered copy of this License. I. Preserve the section Entitled "History", Preserve its Title, and add to it an item stating at least the title, year, new authors, and publisher of the Modified Version as given on the Title Page. If there is no section Entitled "History" in the Document, create one stating the title, year, authors, and publisher of the Document as given on its Title Page, then add an item describing the Modified Version as stated in the previous sentence. J. Preserve the network location, if any, given in the Document for public access to a Transparent copy of the Document, and likewise the network locations given in the Document for previous versions it was based on. These may be placed in the "History" section. You may omit a network location for a work that was published at least four years before the Document itself, or if the original publisher of the version it refers to gives permission. K. For any section Entitled "Acknowledgements" or "Dedications", Preserve the Title of the section, and preserve in the section all the substance and tone of each of the contributor acknowledgements and/or dedications given therein. L. Preserve all the Invariant Sections of the Document, unaltered in their text and in their titles. Section numbers or the equivalent are not considered part of the section titles. M. Delete any section Entitled "Endorsements". Such a section may not be included in the Modified Version. N. Do not retitle any existing section to be Entitled "Endorsements" or to conflict in title with any Invariant Section. O. Preserve any Warranty Disclaimers. If the Modified Version includes new front-matter sections or appendices that qualify as Secondary Sections and contain no material copied from the Document, you may at your option designate some or all of these sections as invariant. To do this, add their titles to the list of Invariant Sections in the Modified Version's license notice. These titles must be distinct from any other section titles. You may add a section Entitled "Endorsements", provided it contains nothing but endorsements of your Modified Version by various parties--for example, statements of peer review or that the text has been approved by an organization as the authoritative definition of a standard. You may add a passage of up to five words as a Front-Cover Text, and a passage of up to 25 words as a Back-Cover Text, to the end of the list of Cover Texts in the Modified Version. Only one passage of Front-Cover Text and one of Back-Cover Text may be added by (or through arrangements made by) any one entity. If the Document already includes a cover text for the same cover, previously added by you or by arrangement made by the same entity you are acting on behalf of, you may not add another; but you may replace the old one, on explicit permission from the previous publisher that added the old one. The author(s) and publisher(s) of the Document do not by this License give permission to use their names for publicity for or to assert or imply endorsement of any Modified Version.

5. COMBINING DOCUMENTS
You may combine the Document with other documents released under this License, under the terms defined in section 4 above for modified versions, provided that you include in the combination all of the Invariant Sections of all of the original documents, unmodified, and list them all as Invariant Sections of your combined work in its license notice, and that you preserve all their Warranty Disclaimers. The combined work need only contain one copy of this License, and multiple identical Invariant Sections may be replaced with a single copy. If there are multiple Invariant Sections with the same name but different contents, make the title of each such section unique by adding at the end of it, in parentheses, the name of the original author or publisher of that section if known, or else a unique number. Make the same adjustment to the section titles in the list of Invariant Sections in the license notice of the combined work. In the combination, you must combine any sections Entitled "History" in the various original documents, forming one section Entitled "History"; likewise combine any sections Entitled "Acknowledgements", and any sections Entitled "Dedications". You must delete all sections Entitled "Endorsements".

6. COLLECTIONS OF DOCUMENTS
You may make a collection consisting of the Document and other documents released under this License, and replace the individual copies of this License in the various documents with a single copy that is included in the collection, provided that you follow the rules of this License for verbatim copying of each of the documents in all other respects. You may extract a single document from such a collection, and distribute it individually under this License, provided you insert a copy of this License into the extracted document, and follow this License in all other respects regarding verbatim copying of that document.

7. AGGREGATION WITH INDEPENDENT WORKS
A compilation of the Document or its derivatives with other separate and independent documents or works, in or on a volume of a storage or distribution medium, is called an "aggregate" if the copyright resulting from the compilation is not used to limit the legal rights of the compilation's users beyond what the individual works permit. When the Document is included in an aggregate, this License does not apply to the other works in the aggregate which are not themselves derivative works of the Document. If the Cover Text requirement of section 3 is applicable to these copies of the Document, then if the Document is less than one half of the entire aggregate, the Document's Cover Texts may be placed on covers that bracket the Document within the aggregate, or the electronic equivalent of covers if the Document is in electronic form. Otherwise they must appear on printed covers that bracket the whole aggregate.

8. TRANSLATION
Translation is considered a kind of modification, so you may distribute translations of the Document under the terms of section 4. Replacing Invariant Sections with translations requires special permission from their copyright holders, but you may include translations of some or all Invariant Sections in addition to the original versions of these Invariant Sections. You may include a translation of this License, and all the license notices in the Document, and any Warranty Disclaimers, provided that you also include the original English version of this License and the original versions of those notices and disclaimers. In case of a disagreement between the translation and the original version of this License or a notice or disclaimer, the original version will prevail. If a section in the Document is Entitled "Acknowledgements", "Dedications", or "History", the requirement (section 4) to Preserve its Title (section 1) will typically require changing the actual title.

9. TERMINATION
You may not copy, modify, sublicense, or distribute the Document except as expressly provided for under this License. Any other attempt to copy, modify, sublicense or distribute the Document is void, and will automatically terminate your rights under this License. However, parties who have received copies, or rights, from you under this License will not have their licenses terminated so long as such parties remain in full compliance.

10. FUTURE REVISIONS OF THIS LICENSE
The Free Software Foundation may publish new, revised versions of the GNU Free Documentation License from time to time. Such new versions will be similar in spirit to the present version, but may differ in detail to address new problems or concerns. See http://www.gnu.org/copyleft/. Each version of the License is given a distinguishing version number. If the Document specifies that a particular numbered version of this License "or any later version" applies to it, you have the option of following the terms and conditions either of that specified version or of any later version that has been published (not as a draft) by the Free Software Foundation. If the Document does not specify a version number of this License, you may choose any version ever published (not as a draft) by the Free Software Foundation. ADDENDUM: How to use this License for your documents To use this License in a document you have written, include a copy of the License in the document and put the following copyright and license notices just after the title page: Copyright (c) YEAR YOUR NAME. Permission is granted to copy, distribute and/or modify this document under the terms of the GNU Free Documentation License, Version 1.2 or any later version published by the Free Software Foundation; with no Invariant Sections, no Front-Cover Texts, and no Back-Cover Texts. A copy of the license is included in the section entitled "GNU Free Documentation License". If you have Invariant Sections, Front-Cover Texts and Back-Cover Texts, replace the "with...Texts." line with this: with the Invariant Sections being LIST THEIR TITLES, with the Front-Cover Texts being LIST, and with the Back-Cover Texts being LIST. If you have Invariant Sections without Cover Texts, or some other combination of the three, merge those two alternatives to suit the situation. If your document contains nontrivial examples of program code, we recommend releasing these examples in parallel under your choice of free software license, such as the GNU General Public License, to permit their use in free software.

Printed by Books on Demand GmbH, Norderstedt / Germany